WHO CUT THE CHEESE?

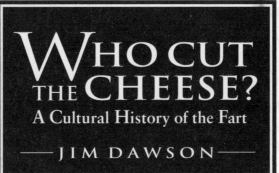

WHO CUT
THE CHEESE?

A Cultural History of the Fart

—— JIM DAWSON ——

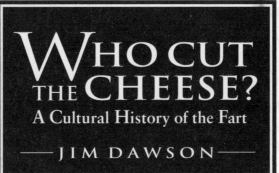

10

TEN SPEED PRESS
Berkeley

Ten Speed Press and the Ten Speed Press colophon
are registered trademarks of Random House, Inc.

Cover and interior design by Gary Bernal
Cover photo from Explorer Paris/Superstock:
Detail from *Thirty-Six Faces of Expression*, by Louis Boilly.

Library of Congress Cataloging-in-Publication Data
on file with the publisher.

ISBN-13: 978-158008-011-8

Printed in Canada

22 21 20 19 18 17 16 15 14 13

First Edition

Alas!
This book of gas
has come to pass:
Who Cut the Cheese?

   —Haiku

CONTENTS

ACKNOWLEDGMENTS

Thanks to Hal Ackerman, Robin Banks, Ray Baxter, Adam & Kathy Birket, Marc Bland, Eddie Brandt, Ray Campi, Romeo T. Carey, Solis Cooperson, Doctor Demento (Barret Hansen), Martin Devane, J. T. Doggett, Jacquelene Edwards, Art & Jennifer Fein, Susan Fogely, Sam Frank, Mikal Gilmore, Diane Heller, Skip Heller, Manuel & Carmen Jimenez, Kate Karp, Tommy Lamey, Allen Larman, Johnny Legend, Golden Bill Liebowitz, Jackie "Jokeman" Martling, Harry Narunsky, Opel & Ellen Nations, Alice Nichols, Joy Nolan, Lyn Nystrom, Michael Ochs, Kendall Overlid, Howard J. Patterson, Lew Pipes, Guy Pohlman, Hallie & Olivia Pootwell, Eric Predoehl, Steve Propes, Omid Rahmanian, my editor Jason Rath, Ray Regalado, Eric Reinhalter, Jeff Riley, Lew Sleeman, John Sneddon, Pat Stutsman, John Waters, my agent Frank Weimann, Ian Whitcomb, Bill Womack, and the many fine folks at the Central Los Angeles Library and the Hollywood Library for the assistance they gave to this project.

If anyone has a good fart fact, fart story or fart joke that can be added to a future edition of this book, please send it to The Gasworks at 1608 N. Cahuenga Boulevard #442, Hollywood, CA 90028.

For those reviewers who can't find words to describe this book, you have my permission to use any of the blurbs below. But please, only one blurb per reviewer.

"The publisher has a real stinker on its hands!"

"Dawson has exhausted his subject!"

"The author should've kept this book on the back burner!"

"A pocket of methane within the bowels of the publishing industry!"

"Certainly one book I don't plan to bury my nose in!"

ACKNOWLEDGMENTS

"Should keep the Literary Establishment fuming!"
"As a cheesy writer, Dawson doesn't quite cut it!"
"Breaks no new ground but...!"
"Wait'll the public gets wind of this book!"
"A chronicle of life on the cutting-cheese edge!"

INTRODUCTION

The question people ask me the most is, "What made you want to write a book about farts?" Well, as with most inspirations and wild ideas, it just bubbled up into consciousness one evening.

I was sitting in the bathtub at the time.

Why, I wondered, were farts so damned funny? It wasn't just me. Guys always seemed to be making light of them, or *actually* lighting them, or letting them at inappropriate times. It was a revelation when, during my first college reading of Geoffrey Chaucer's *Canterbury Tales* in the late 1960s, I stumbled upon the elaborate fart jokes he created 600 years ago. About that same time I was introduced to that august collection of tomes, the Oxford English Dictionary, an anal-retentive etymologist's delight. Looking up the word *fart* (along with a couple of other equally disreputable words), I was surprised to discover not only the numerous examples of how the word has fared over the centuries, but also how painstakingly the editors dwelled on them. My direction in life was set: Someday I would write a fart book—no, not just *a* fart book, *the* fart book—so definitive that millions of people would throw all their other fart books away.

To tell you the truth, I have no recollection of ever passing gas as a child. I don't even remember if my family had a pet name for farting. But I must have done it, because I remember being afraid—being *very* afraid—of letting one slip in church during my gut-wrenching stint as an altar boy, armed with a noisy bronze candle lighter/snuffer, sitting conspicuously in the first row, in front of God and everybody, and keenly aware that the hard, wooden pews had a way of trumpeting every thump and clatter like a bullhorn.

My three most memorable farts occurred after I had become an adult and should have known better. The first one was easily the funni-est. I was stationed at an infantry training base near Camp Lejeune,

North Carolina, and was fond of spending my evenings at the taverns outside the gate, on Route 17, flirting with Asian barmaids, drinking cheap Falstaff beer, and eating pickled eggs out of the type of jars that circuses once reserved for two-headed babies. One morning, after a particularly rough night, I walked into the C.O.'s outer office, let off a silent but deadly, and hurried out again. Within moments I heard a barrage of choking and angry shouts, as if the office staff had been hit by a tear gas canister. I laughed about that for months.

The second fart happened in Cape May, New Jersey, while I was walking down a narrow side street with my friend Mike McHenry. I blasted a roaring number that must have created a bubble in the seat of my pants, if not an outright brown stain. Suddenly a twinge of paranoia made me glance over my shoulder. Not more than six feet behind us were two young, attractive girls who only moments before had stepped out of a doorway and into our wake. I was quick-witted enough to glare accusingly at Mike and call him a rotten bastard, but I still turned red with embarrassment—and, as you can see, that moment haunts me even now. I wonder if the two girls remember it.

FART HUMOR

"The drawback with fart humor," says humorist Garrison Keillor, "is that it's improvisational by nature, and it loses a lot in the telling. You had to be there!"

Although Keillor was speaking of the hilarity of an actual fart, fart humor of all kinds can give us tremendous insights into our cultural fears and values. Since it flouts society's powerful taboos against any expression of our bodily functions, crepitation comedy can break the taboos' hold on both ourselves and our listeners. Fart humor dissipates some of the stress from the self-disgust that our parents drummed into our toddler psyches during the rigors of toilet training. Otherwise, why would anybody burst out laughing at comments about odorous air escaping from someone's asshole—much less at the air itself?

Fart humor takes many forms, including schoolyard chants ("Beans, beans, the musical fruit, the more you eat the more you toot. . . ."), bathroom graffiti ("Here I sit all brokenhearted, tried to shit but only farted"), puns ("I think that last fart exhausted the subject"), retorts ("Did something just crawl up inside you and die?"), and rejoinders to those retorts ("You smelt it, you dealt it"). Very little of this is actually clever or funny, because it's mostly canned humor and good only once per person. But that doesn't seem to stop us from repeating these dry old cracks.

The most common form of humor, however, is fart jokes—little stories with surprise endings—that guys of all ages tell at school, at work, and over a round of beers, and some of these jokes have been scattered throughout this book for your enjoyment.

The third memorable fart occurred in the front seat of a car, during what amounted to an impromptu three-way farting contest as a couple of buddies and I drove down Normandie Avenue in Los Angeles. Gritting my teeth and trying desperately to keep up my end, so to speak, I succeeded only in drawing a little mud. It was a wet one. All right, I almost shit in my pants! I was thirty-five at the time—much too old to be farting around like an adolescent. That episode remains a constant source of self-recrimination that will cling to me, like the stench of a Falstaff beer fart, until the day I die.

I've always wondered why guys generally get a big kick out of farts, but women glare down their noses at them. I'm sure that this female disdain isn't genetic. One of my friend's preschool daughters once farted in my lap and giggled uproariously about it. And not long ago I watched a sweet little four-year girl run through a room announcing, "I farted! I farted!" In her 1996 bestseller, *Divine Secrets of the Ya-Ya Sisterhood*, Rebecca Wells even wrote an entire chapter about a class of eight-year-old Louisiana girls at a Shirley Temple look-alike contest laughing and hooting over their classmate's proud, on-stage poot. But somewhere around the third grade all these little girls morph into miniature schoolmarms, ready to aim their scorn at any squeak or squib emanating from the human body.

Little boys conform too, but in the process they learn to treasure the fart's subversive power. They come to know that a well-timed fart, especially one bounced off the right surface, can disrupt a class; that a well-blamed fart can get another kid in trouble; and that a fart injected into the right moment—say, the silence between *aah* and *men* at the end of a hymn or during a sappy Leonardo DiCaprio love scene—can make a kid an instant hero with the other guys.

During my high school senior year, my buddy Joe Ewing taught me how to mimic farts by squeezing my palms together. It was a dangerous technique to literally put into the hands of an immature seventeen-year-old kid, for within the week my disruptive noises in study hall led to a three-day expulsion from school. I had found my calling.

Thanks to this book, I can safely say that I have probably generated more embarrassment about farting than any other modern human being because, for well over a year during my research, I needed to be an inquisitive cultural anthropologist. I began my field study by asking friends about their farts, the words their families used for farts, their feelings about farts, their funniest fart jokes and stories, and their favorite literary and cinematic farts. From there I moved on to acquaintances . . . then to strangers. At some point I would turn nearly every conversation—whether in a coffee shop, in a waiting room, in a bar, at a party, at the gym, or on a dinner date—into a scatological inquiry.

Before long I became, at least in polite quarters, a pariah whose very presence could get people whispering behind their hands. Women crinkled their noses and rolled their eyes when they saw me coming. The reeking fumes of reproach followed me around like huge black flies, and some people began to ask if I was losing my marbles. Literary-minded people dismissed my efforts altogether and told me that a book about farting wouldn't be worth a hill of beans.

But thank goodness, along came Ten Speed Press to save the day. Faced with the tough choice of either publishing *Who Cut the Cheese?* or pouring their money down a rat hole, they decided to go with the former. Now, perhaps, I'll be redeemed somehow and folks will think my work had a good purpose and was worthwhile after all.

—Jim Dawson, Fartologist

WHO CUT THE CHEESE?

1

ALL GOD'S CHILDREN
GOTTA FART

Love is the fart of every heart;
It pains a man when 'tis kept close,
and others doth offend when 'tis let loose.

—*Sir John Suckling,*
"Loving and Beloved" (1640)

First of all, let me say that a fart is puny, transitory, and evanescent. A turd can fossilize into a coprolite permanent enough to reveal its creator's dietary habits to distant future generations, but a fart, no matter how uproarious, slips immediately into history, never to be smelled or heard from again. No mud or amber has ever trapped it. I've heard rumors that there are corked vials containing gas from such personages as Abraham Lincoln and Marilyn Monroe, but no such relic whose origin could be authenticated has ever turned up.

Yet the fart remains with us, lurking just over our shoulders.

Whoops, there goes one now.

To the ancient Greeks, our Western cultural ancestors, farting was low comedy, but comedy nonetheless. Aristophanes, one of the greatest of the early Athenian playwrights, amused the huge audiences at the Dionysian festivals on the southern slope of the Acropolis with occasional flatulence jokes. In one of his popular plays, *Frogs* (written in 405 B.C.), Aristophanes addressed the issue of fart humor directly in the opening scene when Dionysus, the god of wine and song, led his servant Xanthias, sitting on a donkey, onto the stage:

XANTHIAS [surveying the crowd]: What about one of the old gags, sir? I can always get a laugh with those.

DIONYSUS: All right, Xanthias, but don't just keep saying, "What a load." I've got enough to put up with as it is.

XANTHIAS: Something a bit wittier, eh, sir?

DIONYSUS: Yes, but don't start off with "Oh, my poor neck!"

XANTHIAS: Oh, too bad. What can I give them? Oh, you mean something really funny?

DIONYSUS: Yes, and I don't mean just shifting that pole around and saying you want to *ease yourself* of a—

XANTHIAS: Well, how about this: "If nobody will take away my pack, I'll let a fart and blow it off my back."

DIONYSUS: Keep that one until I really need to puke.

The first-century Roman poet Martial agreed with Xanthias. "I would prefer that you fart," he wrote in *Epigrams XII, 77*, "because . . . that would be useful, and, at the same time, it stimulates laughter."

Flatulence remained a highly regarded source of humor throughout most of European history, especially among the lower classes. Only in the eighteenth century did moral authorities begin to actively suppress it. Since then, Great Britain and America in particular have had a difficult time dealing with the fart. Scientists have tried to cure the fart; etiquette books admonished against it;

Zeke decides it's time to build a new outhouse because the present one is so rotten that it might fall over at any moment. He has a little dynamite left over from blowing out tree stumps a few days earlier, so he wires it up under the old shithouse and tells his family to stay away.

Unfortunately, ol' Granny doesn't get the news. Feeling a case of the barnyard trots, she hurries out back and is sitting contentedly on the oval, gazing out through the quarter-moon hole, when Zeke touches the wires to his battery and blows everything sky high.

After Granny lands a dozen feet away in a puddle of shit, she sits up, gets her bearings, straightens her wig and exclaims, "Whooo-eee! I'm glad I didn't let that one in the house!"

Victorian ladies rustled their bustles to camouflage its sound; publishers hid it behind euphemisms or censored it altogether; and bluenoses declared farting a sin.

Even as the new millennium arrives, farting is still such an anathema that people worry about its effects on their jobs, reputations, and love lives. Believe it or not, many folks resort to the subterfuge of sneaking out farts and then, eyes coyly perusing the ceiling, acting as innocent as bunny rabbits, hoping someone else will be blamed. But in intimate situations no one else can be accused—and so the devil must pay. *The New York Times* reported in 1995 that some couples were even inserting clauses against farting in their prenuptial agreements.

Our taboo against farting is part of our taboo against shit. Everything we eat turns to shit or internal gas, yet we act as if turds and farts don't exist. In his foreword to the 1913 reprint of John G. Bourke's *Scatalogic Rites of All Nations*, the father of psychiatry, Sigmund Freud, wrote:

> [Civilized men] are clearly embarrassed by anything that
> reminds them too much of their animal origin. They are try-
> ing to emulate the "more perfect angels" in the last scene of
> *Faust*, who complain: "For us there remains a trace of the
> Earth embarrassing to bear. . . ." [We] have chosen to evade
> the predicament by . . . denying the very existence of this
> inconvenient "trace of the Earth" [and] concealing it from
> one another, and by withholding from it the attention and
> care which it might claim as an integrating component of
> [our] essential being.

Strict, even fatal, proscriptions against farting have existed in all kinds of cultures. In a commentary within his translation of *The Arabian Nights*, British explorer Richard Burton observed in the 1880s: "The [Bedouin], who [burps] as a matter of civility, has a mortal hatred to a *crepitus ventris*; and were a bystander to laugh at its accidental occurrence, he would at once be cut down as a [point of honor]. The same is the custom amongst the Highlanders of Afghanistan." Captain Richard Jobson, who explored Africa's

Gambia River in 1619–20, wrote that members of the Ashanti tribe on the Gold Coast "are very careful not to let a fart, if anybody be by them. They wonder at our Netherlanders that use it so commonly, for they cannot abide that a man should fart before them, esteeming it to be a great shame and contempt done unto them." One old man of the tribe felt so disgraced by having farted as he bowed to his chief that he hanged himself within the hour. Scottish explorer David Livingstone (of "Dr. Livingstone I presume" fame) reported in 1865 that several African tribes, which tolerated flatulence among themselves, ostracized their members for farting in the presence of strangers. And anthropologist Bronislaw Malinowski remarked in the 1920s that the Trobriand Islanders of Melanesia, who believed that powerful magical spells entered the nose, considered the odor of a fart a dangerous intrusion upon them.

Certainly the fart has long been a crude way to express contempt. In 1610, playwright Ben Jonson wrote in the opening scene of his most popular comedy, *The Alchemist*, "I fart at thee!" John Crowne, in *Sir Courtly Nice* (1685), dismissed an adversary with "A fart for your family!" The Dutch humanist Erasmus opined in the early sixteenth century that "I cannot sufficiently admire that there are not some who fart against these men." Even in modern times, American poet e.e. cummings quipped in a 1925 poem, "No Thanks," that "at him they fart they fart full oft." In two extreme examples of the fart as an insult, the Greek historian Herodotus chronicled the adventures of the Egyptian general Amasis, who farted at his king's envoy and told him to take that message back to the court; and the Jewish historian Josephus reported an incident of a Roman soldier sparking a deadly revolt in Jerusalem by farting at Passover worshippers. (For more details on these latter two events, see the sidebars on pages 8 and 27.)

Doctors have prescribed a good fart for robust health for several thousand years. The Greek physician Hippocrates, for whom modern medicine's Hippocratic oath was named, wrote in 420 B.C., "It is best for flatulence to pass without noise a-breaking, though it is better for it to pass with noise than to be intercepted and accumulated internally." "The fart as much as the burp must be permitted in the same way," the Roman philosopher Cicero said in a private letter to Paetus in the first century B.C. When Claudius became Roman emperor in A.D. 41, according to Suetonius Tranquillus, he "planned an edict to legitimize the breaking of wind at table [at banquets], either silently or noisily, after hearing about a man who was so modest that he endangered his health by an attempt to restrain himself." Claudius's contemporary, Gaius Petronius, made a similar diagnosis in his work *Satyricon*: "Take my word for it, friends, the vapors go straight to your brain. Poison your whole system. I know some who've died from being too polite and holding it in."

A thousand years later, in the eleventh century, four doctors who ran the school of Salerno near the Gulf of Naples came up with a fart-friendly health code after years of treating what they considered the ill effects of "wind held in." According to this code, "Those who suppress [farts] risk dropsy, convulsions, vertigo and frightful colics. These are too often the unhappy outcome of a sad discretion." French essayist Michel de Montaigne, bemoaning his own constipation in an update of his "Of the Power of the Imagination" (1595), lamented, "And would to God that I knew only from the history books how often our stomach, by the refusing of one single fart, may bring us to the very gates of a most excruciating death. And if only that emperor [Claudius] who gave us liberty to fart in any place had also given us the power to do so." Elizabethan poet and dramatist John Heywood wrote in 1556, "What winde can there blow, that doth not some men please? A fart in the blowyng doth the blower ease." Finally, Sir Thomas More, the man for all seasons who gave us *Utopia*, summed it all up in verse, with a political statement tagged on for good measure, when he wrote in a 1518 epigram called "On Breaking Wind" (*In Efflatum Ventris*), "Wind, if you keep it too long in your stomach, kills you; on the other hand, it can save your life if it is properly let out. If wind can save or destroy you, then is it not as powerful as dreaded kings?" In More's case, the answer was no, for King Henry VIII would later behead him.

Unlike the other four senses located in the logical regions of the forebrain, our sense of smell is wired directly into the limbic system, the so-called "reptilian" cellar of the brain responsible for our most basic emotions, from rage to lust. Many anthropologists believe that human civilization would have been impossible if our ancestors hadn't first lost their hypersensitivity to the scents of sex, violence, and territorial marking. That may explain why we treat smell as our lowest sense. Vision is associated with clarity and pre-science. Touch is often said to be magical or golden, soft or light or delicate. Taste can mean refinement. But we smell a rat, the whole rotten business reeks to high heaven, get a whiff of that, it smells fishy to me, it's nothing to sniff at, he's a real stinker, *whoooooooo-eeee*! Perhaps we began turning up our noses at fetid stenches in the Middle Ages, when philosophers, surrounded by a landscape of dunghills, open sewers, and cesspools, deemed our olfactory sense to be vulgar because it didn't contribute to human intellect or bring us the world's beauty. The best our noses could do was alert us to the air's deadly corruption, which created the diseases and plagues that fell upon mankind every few years. By the eighteenth century an entire branch of science centered in France began to concern itself with the effects of "airs" on health; one medical observer, Boissier de Sauvages, wrote in 1746 that when men "breathe the stinking blasts exhaled by the stomachs of oxen . . . , they are attacked by colics, followed by vomiting, and even diarrhea." British poet John Milton had already remarked upon the problem a century earlier, in *Lycidas* (1637): "The hungry sheep look up, and are not fed. But, swoln with wind and the rank mist they draw, rot inwardly and foul contagion spread."

We who live in modern societies spend a great deal of time expunging our environments of odors and replacing them with fragrances. (Scientists tell us the human nose can detect about 10,000 odors.) We keep our water running to avoid stagnancy. We spend billions of dollars each year making our bodies redolent of soap, deodorants, perfumes, colognes, talcums, aftershave lotions, and douches, trying to smell like something other than ourselves. When we're not ventilating our cars, homes, and offices, we scent them with chemicals mimicking pine needles, lemons, and sea air. And though we generate unprecedented amounts of personal garbage and effluvia, our furtive drainage systems carry it all away to be sanitized and dumped far beyond our sensitive nostrils.

No wonder the fart is such an unwelcome and shocking guest.

But over the past decade, farting in America and Great Britain has, to some extent, come out into the open air. We've publicly acknowledged that farts are funny. Children's books have begun to discuss "the gas we pass," greeting cards make light of farts, talk-show hosts joke about them, and TV and film comedies routinely turn farts into gags. Radio host Howard Stern farts almost daily into the microphone to amuse his listeners across North America.

But should farting be allowed to become commonplace? As the Roman philosopher Lucretius pictured it a couple of millennia ago, odorous objects (in this case farts) are made up of "corpuscles" that enter other people's noses like a vaporized spirit and create a union in the mucous, thus chemically melding person A's fart with person B's body—not a pretty picture. Lucretius's science wasn't far off the mark. A fart's molecules go to the mucous lining at the top of your nose, whereupon they are transported to millions of receptor cells in the membrane lining. There the farty molecules are transmuted into electrical signals that travel along a corridor of nerve fibers into your brain. You and somebody's stray fart have now bonded and become one—and I'm glad it's you and not me.

Perhaps the notion of proud, feel-good farting is not in the best interests of society. After all, who wants to smell your farts—besides you?

Reading about farts, though, that's something else. The world of farting is wider, grander, and more interesting than you might have imagined.

A FART LED TO THE DEATH OF THOUSANDS!

In the ancient kingdom of Judea, a fart during Passover ignited a bloody Jewish revolt against Roman occupation troops, according to the Jewish-Roman historian Flavius Josephus in book two of his *The Wars of the Jews*, written in A.D. 75. Shortly after the death of King Herod in A.D. 44, Josephus wrote that

> The Jews' ruin came on, for when the multitudes were come together to Jerusalem, to the feast of unleavened bread, and a Roman cohort stood over the cloisters of the temple (for they always were armed and kept guard at the festivals, to prevent any innovation which the multitude thus gathered together might take), one of the soldiers pulled back his garment, and cowering down after an indecent manner, turned his breech [ass] to the Jews, and spoke such words as you might expect upon such a posture.
>
> At this the whole multitude had indignation, and made a clamor to Cumanus [the provincial Roman procurator], that he would punish the soldier; while the rasher part of the youth, and such as were naturally the most tumultuous, fell to fighting, and caught up stones, and threw them at the soldiers.
>
> Upon which Cumanus was afraid lest all the people should make an assault upon him, and sent to call for more armed men, who, when they came in great numbers into the cloisters, the Jews were in a very great consternation; and being beaten out of the temple, they ran into the city; and the violence with which they crowded to get out was so great, that they trod upon each other, and squeezed one another, till ten thousand of them were killed, insomuch that this feast became the cause of mourning to the whole nation, and every family lamented.

2

THE FART

Reader, it was born, and cry'd,
crack'd so, smelt so, and so dy'd.

—*Sir John Mennis,*
"A Fart's Epitaph" (1656)

All right, this gets a little technical, but I'm only gonna say it once, so pay attention and read carefully. Just as a jet engine turns kerosene fuel into a loud scream, you create a fart by converting undigested food in your lower colon into intestinal gas and then blowing it through a small aperture where the fatty flaps and folds of the integument—the brown part of the rectum's mucous membrane—vibrate and often create a fleshy clamor. The more you push and squeeze, the louder the fart sounds.

The fart is created mostly by *E. coli* and other bacteria in your intestine that feast upon fermenting food and then collectively microfart it inside you; the air you swallow and your stomach's alkaline secretions also have an effect on your farts. On the average a fart is composed of about 59 percent nitrogen, 21 percent hydrogen, 9 percent carbon dioxide, 7 percent methane, and 4 percent oxygen—all of which are odorless. But less than 1 percent of a fart is made up of tiny amounts of other chemicals—such as ammonia and skatole (from the Greek *skatos*, meaning shit)—that stink so pungently, people can smell them at levels of 1 part in 100 million parts of air; if the Pentagon could concentrate *that* into a gas compound, we wouldn't need nuclear weapons. Often hydrogen sulfide, coming mostly from mucous, is added to the mixture, lending the fart a scent of rotten eggs. (In fact, there's a guy at the Veterans Administration hospital in Minneapolis named Dr. Michael Levitt who says sulfur is the fart's worst feature.)

With the right mixture of hydrogen, oxygen, and methane, a fart resembles ordinary swamp gas—volatile and combustible enough to create a mild explosion. If you hold a match up to your anus when the fart's on its way out, the flame will turn blue, flare up, and amuse your buddies. If it's really potent, it'll singe the hair off your ass.

The temperature of your fart is 98.6 degrees Fahrenheit, just like you or one of your turds, until you release it, at which point it can blow hot or cold, depending on whether you've let it off in a windstorm or a Jacuzzi. Once out in the world, the fart darts away from "ground zero" at a speed that's been clocked at ten feet per second. That's much faster than fog, which can only creep on little cat feet.

If you seem to be chronically plagued by farts, you're in good company with thirty million other Americans who, according to the fainthearted, fart too much. That's more than 10 percent of the population. Lately farting has become much more common because we're adding fiber to our diets. The most common foods that create farts are milk products, dried beans and peas, cucumbers, oat bran, cabbage, raw broccoli, brussels sprouts, unfermented soybean foods, raw carrots, onions, celery, apples, bananas (especially green ones), apricots, watermelon, fatty meats, high-fiber cereals, chestnuts, bread, and pasta. Tap water also adds to the mix if it contains a lot of chemicals, and carbonated drinks like soda pop—well, I shouldn't have to tell you what effect those have.

If you're a guy and you eat a fairly healthy diet, you release about a quart of gas every day, parceled out over an average of ten to fifteen farts, varying in magnitude. In 1976, the *New England Journal of Medicine* reported on a Minnesota patient who, over a period of five years, averaged thirty-four farts a day. During one four-hour period he blasted seventy farts. His daily record was 141.

He had very few friends. Women fart less, about eight or nine times a day. Sometimes you may not even be aware you farted. As you get older you'll find yourself farting with greater frequency, because your bowels become less elastic and thus less likely to store up gas. Generally the gas accumulates during the day and escapes at bedtime, when you're relaxing. You may even pull the covers over your head in order to savor the gas's delicate bouquet more fully.

Some people turn their noses up at the mere mention of a fart, but farting's pretty indispensable. Without farting, you're in a world of shit, my friend. Gas trapped in your colon's various right-angled turns can cause severe pains throughout your chest and arms that resemble the symptoms of a heart attack. Chronic distention of the bowels can create all sorts of health problems. If gas is kept prisoner for too long, it can make your life miserable. Two scientists in Holland announced in 1994 that for good health you need to fart about fifteen times a day, whether you want to or not.

Sometimes you're probably embarrassed when people around you confuse a borborygmi, the gurgling sound of air bubbles passing through liquids in your small intestine, with a fart. Ashamed that somebody might think it's a fart (when in fact it's only a nascent fart waiting to happen down the line), you'll often say your stomach is growling.

Probably the most common sources of farting are three complex sugars—raffinose, stachyose, and verbacose—more commonly called oligosaccharides, dubbed by clinical researchers as the "flatulent factors." Oligosaccharides are found in most green vegetables and legumes, but the vegetable kingdom's poster boy for flatulence, the one that usually takes the rap and gets all the bad press, is the common bean, or *Phaseolus vulgaris*. Is there really anyone out there, whether you're 6 or 106, who can't recite that old children's rhyme, "Beans, beans, the musical fruit, the more you eat the more you toot, the more you toot the better you feel, beans, beans for every meal"?

A member of the legume family (seeds that grow in pods), the bean is one of nature's perfect foods, at least for humans. It's a little powerhouse of nutrition, bursting with goodness. For example, a cup of dry beans has about sixteen grams of protein but only one gram of mostly unsaturated fat (the "good" kind); sixteen grams of fiber (equal to eight slices of whole-wheat bread); half an adult's daily requirement of folic acid (a B vitamin); and significant amounts of magnesium, copper, potassium, zinc, and iron. The bean has been at the center of most of the world's diet since the beginning of agriculture, many thousands of years ago.

According to *The New York Times*, beans—with their high fiber, low fat, protein abundance, and lack of cholesterol—are becoming more popular each year in the American diet and gaining favor among chefs (except those who prepare airline food). In August 1992, the U.S. Department of Agriculture reported that bean consumption rose to 7.5 pounds per person in 1991, up from 6 pounds the year before and from 5.5 pounds in 1989.

Unfortunately, the bean contains those pesky oligosaccharides. Most of our herbivorous cousins have an enzyme called alpha-galactosidase that breaks down these sugars, but *H. sapiens* don't. When the bean's undigested and unabsorbed sugars move into your large intestine, they're greeted by microbes with a serious sweet tooth. These happy bacteria convert the sugars ("colonic fermentation") and release them in millions of teensy weensy farts as hydrogen and carbon dioxide gases. As these gases expand within your lower intestine and create bloat, they head thunderously for the nearest exit. In other words, fart city.

Before Europeans began colonizing the New World nearly five hundred years ago, they basically had only one bean in their diet: the fava, best known today, thanks to the Hannibal Lecter character in Tim Harris's *Silence of the Lambs*, as a side dish with human liver and a nice Chianti. Though favas are lower in oligosaccharides than many beans, a sizable segment of the populations of Greece and southern Italy has always been allergic to or at least intolerant of them. "One should abstain from fava beans," the Greek philosopher Pythagoras, best known today for his theorem of triangles, advised in the sixth century B.C., "since they are full of wind and take part in the soul, and if one abstains from them one's stomach will be less noisy and one's dreams will be less oppressive and calmer." In any event, many people whose ancestors came from the Mediterranean area still carry the gene that causes fava allergies, generally in the form of acute anemia, which in rare cases can be fatal.

Some say the easiest way to mitigate the bean problem, besides avoiding beans altogether, is to soak them first (leaching out some of the oligosaccharides), discard the water, and then cook them in new water. The aforementioned Dr. Michael Levitt, a Minneapolis gastroenterologist, says that soaking beans can decrease gas in a normal person by one tenth. Other researchers call this an old wives' tale. George Gray, who studied beans for ten years for the U.S. Department of Agriculture in Albany, California, attempted to clear the air once and for all, not by frantically waving his hands but rather by stating: "Whether to soak beans prior to cooking or not is simply a culinary question. It may shorten the cooking time, but other than that, there's no effect [on farting]." He claims that even when beans are boiled and the water then thrown out, the only marked decrease is flavor, not flatulence. If anything helps, Gray adds, it would be to eat *more* beans. "Apparently, if you eat beans regularly, the microflora [in the intestine] adjust somewhat."

People who grow and market other legumes have tried to distance themselves from the bean. "It's not a bean," insists lentil booster Harold Blain of the Indiana-based American Pea and Lentil Association, pointing out that Americans blissfully gobble down thirty-seven million pounds of lentils a year. "Beans have a lot of problems—like, uh, more flatulence—that lentils don't. We think we have a better product."

In the 1970s a food engineer named Benito de Luman, working at the University of California in Berkeley, decided to go to the root of the problem itself by genetically designing a so-called "clean bean" whose oligosaccharides would break down rather than ferment, but somehow this bean did not sprout in the public's imagination.

More recently, British researcher Dr. Colin Leakey, son of anthropologist Louis Leakey, says he has developed a "low-flatulence" bean through his company Peas & Beans, Ltd., of Girton, England. A past winner of the Meritorious Service Award from the Bean Improvement Cooperative, Leakey calls his hybrid the Prim bean because it's more prim and proper than the common "wanton" bean. "I want to improve the consumption of beans as a way of improving nutrition," he told the *Wall Street Journal* in 1997.

While shopping in a Chilean marketplace in 1979, Leakey stumbled upon a less flatulent (and less flavorful) bean known among locals as the "rich man's bean," because it was more expensive. He took samples of this bean back to Europe and over the next decade crossbred it with other varieties to lower their flatulent factors, which Dr. Leakey believes are not oligosaccharides but certain chemicals in bean skins that inhibit human enzymes whose job is to disperse gas into the bloodstream instead of channeling it into the bowels.

You'd think a fartless bean, like a better mousetrap, would have bean lovers beating a path to Leakey's door, but so far he's only been able to sell about $16,000 worth of Prim beans a year. He believes there's a conspiracy working against him. "Big bean companies are worried about marketing low-gas beans because it implies their other beans are high-gas, so it'd be negative marketing," says one of his consultants.

Though Colin Leakey is a fan of his own product, he says he's not part of the antifart crowd. "I have come to the conclusion that flatulence is a very good thing. It's a normal mechanism for ridding oneself of chemicals that can be carcinogenic."

Perhaps the solution is to be found outside of the bean. Since the 1600s, pharmacists and herbalists have used teas, green moss, rosemary, peppermint, cloves, gingerroot, and such agents as activated charcoal (an absorbent), and the drug simethicone (touted to decrease the surface tension of gas bubbles in the intestine) to relieve stomach gas, with mixed, usually negligible, results. But then a dozen or so years ago, an American dairy scientist named Alan Kligerman, who had already developed an enzyme product to help lactose-intolerant people digest milk products, discovered that the fermentation problem could be avoided or at least mitigated by adding a small amount of alpha-galactosidase culture to beans and other gassy foods just before they're eaten. He was convinced that this enzyme would break down oligosaccharides for easy digestion and thus foil the fart. Forthwith, in 1990, Kligerman's company, AkPharma (located, oddly enough, on Old Egg Harbor Road in

Pleasantville, New Jersey), launched an over-the-counter food supplement called Beano that contains alpha-galactosidase extracted from the mold *Aspergillus niger*, which is commonly found on rotting cassavas. Squirted or sprinkled on foods (from three to ten drops per serving), or taken in tablet form, Beano supposedly prevents gas buildup in the intestine. But Beano isn't entirely fartproof. *New York Times* food writer Julie Sahni pointed out that heat can render Beano inactive, eliminating its usefulness when sprinkled or spritzed in soups, stews, and casseroles.

One of AkPharma's biggest challenges was advertising Beano in the straight media without offending people. In late June 1992 it tested an ad in San Francisco and Chicago newspapers that featured exploding fireworks under the headline: "Have a Quiet Fourth." The copy read, "This Fourth of July, eat all the beans and coleslaw and chili and garden fresh vegetables you want. Just remember to use Beano drops first." The company said later that it received almost no complaints. AkPharma had originally planned this campaign a year earlier, but its partner in the ads, a bean canning company, pulled out at the last moment. "It didn't want to be associated with gas," said Beano's marketing manager, Patricia Van Horn. "Gas is one of those subjects that's still taboo."

As with many discoveries, Beano comes equipped with its own unintended consequences. Back in the sixteenth century, a philosopher named John Thurloe wrote that "there are five or six different species of fart." If the AkPharma folks have any say in the matter, their Beano will someday push those five or six species onto the endangered list. We may then have to face the ecological question of whether we really want to drive yet another couple of species, even though they're farts, into extinction.

HITLER GASSED HIMSELF TO DEATH!

According to biographer John Toland, German dictator Adolf Hitler "suffered from meteorism, uncontrollable farting, a condition aggravated by his vegetarianism." Hitler told a doctor in the early 1930s, "The cramps are so severe that sometimes I could scream out loud!" But in 1936 he found solace in a quack Berlin physician named

Theodor Morell, who prescribed a steady dosage of Dr. Koester's Anti-Gas Pills over the next eight years. These nostrums contained extracts of *nux vomica* (a seed containing strychnine) and belladonna (which contains atropine)—in other words, two deadly poisons.

"The Führer ... has had such stomach spasms and gas buildups ever since 1929," Dr. Morell wrote in his diary in 1944. Hitler had originally quelled his gastrointestinal pains with Neo-Balestol, a medical repackaging of World War I gun-cleaning oil that soldiers had used for upset stomach in the trenches. But it contained a poison called fusel oil, and after suffering acute poisoning in 1934, Hitler quit taking Neo-Balestol and ordered it off the market. When Dr. Morell met Hitler two years later, he promised the Nazi leader, "I'll have you healthy again in less than a year."

Morell would later tell Allied interrogators that because of chronic gas trapped in the intestine, Hitler's stomach rang with a drumlike note whenever he (Morell) tapped it with his fingers. According to one memorable notation in Morell's notebook from May 30, 1943: "After eating a vegetable platter, constipation and colossal flatulence occurred on a scale I have seldom encountered before."

By early 1941, when Hitler was directing Germany's invasion of the Soviet Union, he was ingesting "120 to 150 anti-gas pills a week." Finally, in late 1944, an army doctor named Erwin Giesling inquired about the six black little spheres he saw on Hitler's breakfast platter. Checking the ingredients on the flat aluminum can of anti-fart medicine, Dr. Giesling saw that the 120 pills inside contained half a gram of strychnine and half a gram of atropine. He calculated that Hitler had been overdosing himself with poison every day. Checking E. Poulsson's *Handbook of Pharmacology*, Dr. Giesling read that atropine "acts on the central nervous system, first as a stimulant, then as a paralyzer. In humans it primarily affects the forebrain, coupled with vivid flights of ideas, talkativeness, and restlessness, visual and aural hallucinations, and fits of delirium, which may be peaceful and serene but may equally degenerate into acts of violence and frenzy." Strychnine, when taken over a period of time, can create, among other symptoms, euphoria and acute sensitivity to light and sounds. When Dr. Giesling experimented by taking the pills himself, he experienced irritability and extreme sensitivity to stimuli.

Dr. Theodor Morell was relieved of his duties and barely escaped with his own life, but Hitler's health, thanks to his longtime daily blitzkriegs against his own farts, had already declined and his mind had deteriorated. He shot himself in his bunker six months later, in April 1945, as Russian troops were blasting their way into Berlin.

3

WORDS ARE BUT WIND

art! The very word can strike terror into the hearts of proper folks and create a phantom odor strong enough to send them scurrying for cover. Believe me, I've cleared out many rooms with just a murmur, without having to resort to the real thing. Now *that's* the power of language.

Language alone—the Afrikaan's *maagwind* or *poep*, the Israeli's *nuhfeechah* (*nefikhe* in Yiddish), the Japanese's *he*, the Cantonese Chinese's *fong*, the Norwegian's *fjert*, the Swede's *fjart*, the Hollander's *scheet*, the German's *furz*, the Bantu's *lu-suzi*, the Hindu's *pud*, the Pole's *pierdzenic*, the Italian's *peto*, the Russian's *perdun*—tells us that everybody the world over farts. Even Dr. Zamenhoff, who invented the artificial language Esperanto in 1887, recognized the need for a word and came up with *furzo*, a close cousin of the German fart.

Fart has the distinction of being one of the infamous "four-letter words," along with *fuck*, *shit*, *piss*, *cunt*, *cock*, and several other monosyllabic Anglo-Saxonisms unworthy of being spoken in mixed or polite company. (The term *four-letter word* itself dates back to 1929, born in the furor that raged following the publication of D. H. Lawrence's *Lady Chatterley's Lover*.) But *fart's* ignominy has not always been so.

Fart comes from the Old English *verten* (to fart) and *vert* (a fart); when the pronunciation of the consonant *v* shifted into an *f* sound about 600 years ago, *vert* became *fert*. It in turn evolved into *fret*, which besides being colic or a fart (now obsolete) was also an agitation of mind (still current). A fret was also a disagreeable person, known also as a *fretchard*.

The first known appearance of the fart in Old English literature was in the anonymously written poem "The Cuckoo Song," from the year 1250 or thereabouts: "*Bulluc stertess, bucke vertess*"—translated as "the bull leaped, the stag farted"—to express their joy over the coming of summer.

By the nineteenth century the word had been expunged from literature in both Great Britain and the United States, thanks to such prudish editors and reformers as Thomas Bowdler, whose guttings of Shakespeare's bluer passages gave us the word *bowdlerize* (to expurgate). As Bowdler's contemporary, writer Frank Harris, put it, "An old maid's canon of deportment" had repressed the rowdy English tongue. In 1904 Cambridge, England's prim Miss Grace Norton, an authority on Montaigne, elucidated the Victorian mindset when she warned readers in her introduction to his *Essays* that "Montaigne carries his habitual frankness of language to an extreme. . . . It is to be remembered that refinement of language was not insisted upon in his day, and that, in the mind of his contemporaries, his freedom would excite no surprise or displeasure."

Way back in 1755, when Samuel Johnson compiled his groundbreaking *Dictionary of the English Language*, he felt free to define the verb *fart* as "to break wind behind." But already some writers were abbreviating it. As early as 1740, the English poet Thomas Gray felt it necessary to write, "Now they are always in a sweat, and never speak, but they f—t." Satirist Alexander Pope restrained himself in a whimsical poem, "Bounce to Fop, An Heroic Epistle from a Dog at Twickenham to a Dog at Court" (1736), when he wrote, "Fye, naughty Fop! where e'er you come, to f—t and p—ss about the room." And Henry Fielding, in book 7, chapter 3, of his still-popular 1749 novel *The History of Tom Jones*, had Squire Western screaming, "Ho! are you come back to your politics, as for those I despise them as much as I do a f—t." By the late 1800s, when the editors of the massive *Oxford English Dictionary* were putting together a new edition of their volume F, they felt compelled to label *fart* as "Not now in decent use." In the United States, the first (1909) and second (1934) editions of *Webster's New International Dictionary* omitted *fart* altogether; the word wasn't admitted until the third edition in 1961.

Poet John Ciardi commented on the problem in 1954, noting,

> It is worth pointing out that the mention of bodily function is likely to be more shocking in a Protestant than in a Catholic culture. It has always seemed to me that the offensive language of Protestantism is obscenity; the offensive language of Catholicism is profanity or blasphemy: one offends on a scale of unmentionable words for bodily function, the other on a scale of disrespect for the sacred.

Fart itself is a noun, verb, or adjective: He farted a fart and the room smells farty.

In conjunction with other words, it has also developed various pejorative meanings to describe disagreeable or dumb people (an old fart, a silly fart, a stupid fart, a fart-face, a fartknocker). It can signify something worthless ("It doesn't amount to a fart"). A fart blossom is a turd, a particularly horrendous fart odor, or a dummy. A fart-hole in some parts of the United States is a jerk, more commonly referred to as an "asshole." A fartenheimer, taken from the pseudo-German slang word *wisenheimer*, is a wiseass who thinks he's smarter than he actually is.

To fart around, or fiddle-fart around, is to goof off. (The British say "fart about.") A *fart sack* is an army term for a sleeping bag or mattress cover. A fart tunnel, fart funnel, or fart flume is of course the anal canal. A farting spell is a very short time. *Artsy-fartsy* means self-consciously artistic. A farting shot is a fart released as a parting shot, best done while leaving a room or, better yet, an elevator. Acting like a fart in a bottle or a fart in a colander is rushing around in an agitated state, not knowing which hole to come out of. A *brainfart* is an American college expression for a sudden loss of memory; it has evolved among Internet users to mean a mistake created by a mental glitch. Fart breath is just what it says: a serious case of halitosis. Modern American kids, living in a media world of hyperbole, have come up with a name for a really awesome fart: Fartzilla, more horrifying than the fifties Japanese sci-fi icon Godzilla. A pussy fart or cunt fart is either the sucking noise of a well-lubricated vagina as a man withdraws his penis during sexual intercourse or a sound some women can make simply by using their vaginal muscles (showcased to wondrous effect on radio in a 1997 pussy-farting contest on *The Howard Stern Show*). As much chance as a fart in a windstorm is no chance at all; anything *like* a fart in a windstorm is puny and ineffectual.

The British have also been liberal in their use of the word. A fart-catcher, besides being a pederast, can be a personal servant or sycophant—updated from Victorian fartlickers and fartsuckers. *Farting-crackers* is an old expression for trousers. A farting clapper is an anus. Fartleberries are dried bits of shit hanging on butt hairs, which Americans call "dingleberries."

Whether in the United Kingdom or United States, one doesn't just fart. One lets, leaves, lays, cracks, claps, cuts, or rips a fart. Six hundred years ago Geoffrey Chaucer announced, "He let flee a fart!"; more recently, J. D. Salinger wrote, "This guy . . . laid this terrific fart." Laying a fart is patterned on a hen's laying an egg. Ripping a fart comes from its frequent mimicry of the sound of cloth being torn apart. Cutting a fart is probably a back-formation of the phrase "cutting the cheese."

Going back several thousand years to the Indo-European language, the root of nearly all European languages, the earliest known word for passed gas was *perd*, or *pezd*. Vestiges of the *perd* are still with us, such as the Latin *perdix* (the genus word for *partridge*, a bird that makes a whirring sound) and the English *perdition* (damnation, spiritual ruin). *Perd* became the Latin *pedere* (to fart) and *peditum* (a fart), which in turn evolved into the Italian *petto,* the Spanish *pedo,* and the French and Middle English *pet*—the root of the word *petard,* a small, old-fashioned bomb once used to blow holes in fortification walls; the tendency of the petard to misfire and blast its user engendered Shakespeare's oft-repeated line from *Hamlet,* "hoist by his own petard." In Czechoslovakia, Russia, and Denmark the words for fart still sound like *perd.*

In ancient Greece *perd* became *porde,* which still exists in the scientific name *Onopordum acanthium* for cotton thistle, also known as "Scottish thistle," the emblem of Scotland. The name was inspired by this prickly plant's flatulent effect upon certain animals (*onos* means donkey) that grazed upon it.

Since *fart* has long been considered a vulgarism, or *mot cru,* English has had to rely on several fancier words to stand in its place. First there's *crepitate* (to fart), from the Latin *crepitare* (to rattle) and *crepitus ventris* (a fart, literally *crackling wind*), neither of which should be confused with *crap,* short for *crapper,* an early name for the flushable toilet invented by Englishman Thomas Crapper. *Crepitus ventris* survives in English as a dry scientific term.

A more common word in polite company is *flatulence,* from the Latin verb *flare* (to blow). The corresponding Latin noun *flatus* (a fart, literally a *blowing*) was high-falutin' even in Roman times; the common people called a fart a *bumbum* (plural *bumba*), not a *flatus, peditum,* or *crepitus ventris.* The bumbum has survived today through the term *boom-boom,* which we reserve for the farts of small children, along with "stinky" ("Mommy, I went boom-boom" or "I made a stinky").

Flatulence's more common usage as windy blather made it permissible for everyday use, though in 1946 a poll of the National Association of Teachers of Speech found it to be one of the ten worst-sounding words in the English language. Still, *flatulence* is the only word allowed in most newspapers, even to this day. Columnist William Safire calls words like *flatulence* "language of high dudgeon": The trick, he observed, is "to say a word that sounds explosive but is otherwise innocent, or is presumed to be." From flatulence has come the innocent euphemism "full of hot air." But really, what is intestinal hot air but a fart waiting to happen?

Anyway, poor people fart; the rich crepitate or flatulate.

Perhaps the most familiar expression for farting is "breaking wind," which dates back at least to the early sixteenth century, when to break wind meant either to belch or fart, though for farting the words *backwards*, *downwards*, or *behind* were usually added. Thus Shakespeare wrote in *A Comedy of Errors* (1594): "A man may break a word with you, sir; and words are but wind; Ay, and break it in your face, so he break it not behind." (This must be an ancestor of the expression that when you belch, you cheat your ass out of a fart.)

Other common, polite expressions are "passing air," "passing gas," and "passing wind"—all related to the natural passage of food and air through the body before the discharge. The act of passing can also refer to shitting and pissing, depending on what's being passed. The word *pass* here is possibly derived from the Latin stem *pass*, "to suffer"—the source of the word *passion*, which despite its current sexy connotations once referred to the torture and crucifixion of Jesus Christ.

More often the fart goes unnamed or is given a pronoun, such as *it* ("Did you do it?"), *one* ("He let one go!" or "She ripped one off!"), and *them* ("He's been letting them go all night!").

Some former words for fart have taken on new meanings. According to Nathan Bailey's *Universal, Etymological English Dictionary* (1721), the word *poop* meant "to break wind backwards softly," obviously taken from its earlier meaning "to blow or toot, as a horn; a short blast in a hollow tube" (from the Middle English *powpe*). *Poop* would later change into a soft word for shit, both noun and verb, and be replaced in the flatulence lexicon by *poot*—a soft, almost soundless fart—which in turn gave way to *toot*, especially in America. An old poop, incidentally, is an elderly person, usually a man, who would also qualify as being an old fart or a fretchard.

While we're on the subject of poop, there was a Mother Goose nursery rhyme, taken from *Tommy Thumb's Pretty Song Book* (c. 1744), that went: "Little Robin red breast, sitting on a pole, niddle, noddle, went his head, and poop went his hole." *Poop* in this context meant fart. But as the Mother Goose publishers continued to consolidate centuries-old rhymes and stories in newer editions, they cleaned up this particular verse, changing it to: "Little Robin Redbreast, sat upon a rail, niddle, noddle, went his head, wiggle waggle went his tail." Many other rhymes, including "Piss a bed, piss a bed, barley butt, your bum's so heavy, you can't get up," were eliminated altogether.

For the silent fart, an early British word was *fizzle*—"a little, or low-sounding fart," according to a seventeenth-century dictionary. A 1601 translation of Roman historian Pliny the Elder's *Historia naturalis* said that if donkeys ate a certain plant (most likely cotton thistle) "they will fall a fizzling and farting." *Fizzle* has changed since then to mean "to peter out, to fail" or "to make a hissing sound." It has also engendered the shorter, bubbly *fizz*, which linguist Hugh Rawson observed "gives a new meaning to the [old] Alka-Seltzer TV commercial, 'Plop, plop, fizz, fizz, oh what a relief it is'!" *Fizzle*—like the *foist*, the *fice*, and the *fyst* (all early words for hush-hush farts)—comes from the Middle English word *fisten*: "to break wind." As for England's current quiet fart, it's called a "fluff," a "blind fart," or, if it really stinks, "the butler's revenge." In America it's a "whiffer," a "one-cheek sneak," "a slider," "a trouser cough," "a cushion creeper," or if accompanied by a stench out of proportion to its stealth, an "S.B.D" (silent but deadly) or "S.A.V." (silent and violent).

A "rasper" is louder than a "breezer," louder even than the now-defunct British "fartick" and "fartkin." A "rattler," not to mention a "bowel howl," will generally rattle the windows. In Australia an uproarious "gurk" is almost certain to get the kangaroos hopping mad. The "thunder down under" needs no elucidation. But the greatest of all farts, according to artist Salvador Dali, who often wrote about his own farting, was the "double-barreled fart," nearly capable of registering on the Richter scale.

Another kind of fart is the "wet one," venting not only air but water and small amounts of shit; it's also been called a "backfire," because it suggests incomplete combustion. American kids call it a "squidgy," or they'll say they "drew mud." The British call it a "brewer's fart" and the French a "mason's fart" (*pet de macon*)—because it leaves mortar. The wettest fart of all is the "gorp," released underwater as a bubble, usually in a bathtub.

Apparently the use of different names for loud and silent farts is universal: For example, in the Farsi tongue an audible fart is a *gooz*; a silent one a *choas*. An Arabic fart can be an *eegayas* or a *zirt* (loud), an *eezarat* (soft), a *faswah* (silent), or an *eefessy* (silent but deadly).

Euphemisms for farts also generally comment on their smell. The "stinker" is what it says it is. So are the "fat one," the "wallpaper peeler," and the "P.U.," taking its name from the exclamation it elicits from bystanders, not from the Finnish fart, *pieru*. In urban neighborhoods farting is sometimes called "painting the elevator," a term whose origins shouldn't require much explanation. The most common phrase is "cut the cheese," a throwback to the days when cheese was sold in round molds and the first slice through the rind brought forth the pungent odors of fermentation. Smelly farts are also called "cheezers" and "burnt cheese," the latter a condition that has recently been extended to burritos, as when MTV's Butt-head asks his buddy, "Beavis, did you burn another burrito?"

The expressions "to drop a rose" or "pluck a rose" imply through irony an unpleasant stink, as does "floating an air biscuit." The sixteenth-century Dutch painter Hieronymus Bosch included a visual pun on the rose analogy in his famous triptych, *The Garden of Earthly Delights*, showing red roses being expelled from a young lady's ass at the bottom of the central panel. If a fart smells especially bad, an Englishman will want to know, "Did you drop your guts?" or "Did you blow your guts out?" or he may simply tell you, "Don't do that Mogambo in here." A really rotten fart is simply called a "nose closer." An old British Army expression was, "There's a smell of gunpowder," and letting a particularly foul-smelling fart was "burning bad powder." Speaking of burning, a fart that's ignited as it leaves the anus is a "blue dart."

References to farting are often whimsically related to animals and insects, because they're offered to children as euphemisms. "Stepping on a duck (or a frog)" is one; "Was that a barking spider (or a house frog, or a mud cricket)?"; and "Did you shoot a rabbit?" are others, not to mention "Oops, I let Fluffy off the leash." To cover up a fart, folks might ask, "Is there a mouse in here?" (If mice seem inappropriate, some people say the chair is squeaking.) Deer hunters came up with the "bucksnorter," taken from the common query, "Did you hear that buck snort?" "There goes another seagull" is an Irish expression. The animal equivalent to "pull my finger" is to announce, "There's an elephant on my back!"; when the unsuspecting young victim looks to see, he or she is greeted by a trumpeting fart. Another explanation is, "A herd of elephants just ran through here."

One very funny fart is the "flutterbuster," a series of put-put-put-put fartlets that usually comes during jogging, in time to the runner's feet hitting the ground. Over a hundred years ago, Sir Richard Burton wrote in his notes to his translation of *The Arabian Nights* that in the Greek quarter of Cairo he witnessed a flutterbuster, though he didn't call it that, when a group of workers came in from a nearby field: "One had said to the other, 'If thou wilt carry the hoes I will break wind once for every step we take.' He was as good as his word and when they were to part he cried, 'And now for thy bakhshish!' which consisted of a volley of fifty, greatly to the delight of the boys."

Farting is also called "talking German," a reference to the guttural noises common to both farts and the glottal-heavy language of Goethe. London's Cockneys, long known for their secret rhyming slang (stairs, for example, were called "apples and pears" and then shortened to "apples") have been calling loud farts "raspberry tarts," or just "raspberries," since the 1870s. In America the raspberry became the "razzberry," a loud, sputtering imitation of a fart (also called the "Bronx cheer" because of its traditional use by baseball fans against Yankee Stadium umpires) created by sticking the tongue between the lips and making it vibrate against the lower lip by forcefully exhaling air. The fart-sounding razzberry was again shortened to both *berry* ("we gave him the berry") and *razz*—"to tease or heckle." *Razz* is also a noun, as Sinclair Lewis used it in his 1920 novel *Main Street*: "The Red Swede got the razz handed to him." A razzer is a flat rubber toy that makes a wet farting noise when you blow through its wooden mouthpiece. However, "razzle-dazzle"—a noisy and ostentatious display—has other origins and is not related.

Believe it or not, as early as the 1600s, the English even had a term for a cough accompanied by a simultaneous fart: It was a "through-cough." There's even a term for farting in bed and pulling the covers over your head: it's called a "Dutch oven."

Perhaps the most evasive euphemism for farts (along with other body odors) was *vapors*—defined in the *Oxford English Dictionary* as "supposed emanations from internal organs or from substance within the body." "Having the vapors" was a common complaint among women and delicate men in England, and later America, from the sixteenth to the nineteenth centuries. It was a psychosomatic condition that, along with elaborate clothing women wore to trap their odors beneath undergarments, speaks volumes about the profound repression that once existed in bourgeois and upper-class society. In his 1547 medical text, a Dr. Boorde spoke of "a vaporous humour or fumosytie rising from the stomach. It doth nothing lesse then offend the braine . . . with vaporous fumes." Another observer, named Beveridge, wrote in 1729: "These malign vapours which by reason of overmuch eating are exhaled from the stomach into the head." Vapors were considered to be responsible for hysteria, hypochondria, depression, and other nervous disorders.

Finally, you can hardly discuss farts without including the arses, assholes, and bums that vent them. The original English word was *ers*, meaning "wet" in ancient Indo-European. *Ers* became *ars* or *arse* by the eleventh century; then, sometime around the fifteenth century, when an *r* was often dropped if it preceded an *s* (as in *curse, cuss, burst, bust*), *arse* became *ass*, a word already in common usage to denote a certain dumb animal with long ears. However, *arse* is still used in Great Britain, where a popular evasive reply to an inconvenient question is "Ask my arse." We all know what answer the arse will give.

A REVOLT AGAINST THE KING OF EGYPT WAS SOUNDED BY A FART!

According to Greek historian Herodotus, in 569 B.C. King Apries of Egypt sent one of his generals, Amasis, to quell a rebellion among his troops, but when Amasis confronted the mutinous leaders, they put a helmet on his head and declared him the new king. "This was not displeasing to Amasis, as the event showed," Herodotus wrote only a few years later. "For being crowned by the rebels, he made ready to attack Apries. When the king heard of it, he sent Patarbemis, a man of repute and one of his advisors, to bring Amasis alive into his presence. Patarbemis went and summoned Amasis; and he, sitting as it happened upon a horse, raised himself from the saddle and broke wind, bidding [Patarbemis] carry that back to Apries." When the envoy relayed the message (in what form he delivered it was not recorded), King Apries became so enraged that he ordered that Patarbemis's nose and ears be hacked off. This outrageous act of barbarity against such a respected man convinced many Egyptians to join or sympathize with Amasis's growing army.

After Apries was defeated and taken prisoner (and later torn apart by a mob), Amasis became King Ahmose and reigned for forty-four years, from 569 to 525 B.C., which modern historians call one of Egypt's most prosperous periods.

4

LE PETOMANE: THE FINE ART OF FARTING

There once was a fellow from Sparta
A really magnificent farter
On the strength of one bean,
He farted "God Save the Queen,"
And Beethoven's "Moonlight Sonata."

—*Anonymous*

In his 1974 autobiography, director-screenwriter Garson Kanin marveled at his good luck in having worked with John Barrymore, the most prominent member of the American theater's first family, and now best known as Drew Barrymore's grandfather. When Kanin directed Barrymore in a 1939 film called *The Great Man Votes*, he was impressed by the aging actor's ability to deliver tears on cue, including, for dramatic effect, a large tear out of one eye and then, a few seconds later, a salty droplet from the other. After the scene was shot, Barrymore told him, "It's a trick, like being able to blush. Or wiggling your ears. . . . But it isn't acting. It's crying. Doesn't mean a damn thing." Then, according to Kanin, Barrymore added:

> "Some people, you know, can fart at will." He looked troubled. "I've never been able to learn to do that. I'm very disappointed in myself." He laughed his booming laugh. "Did you ever hear of Le Petomane? The great French cabaret performer? That was his act. Farting. He was a tremendous hit. I saw him once when I was a kid. He'd come on and give a sort

of dissertation on the subject and illustrate the different kinds. I remember that for a finish, he farted 'La Marseillaise.' How could I forget it? But I mean to say, I wouldn't call that acting, would you?"

No, but it was a great act that I'd certainly pay to see.

A hundred years ago, a Frenchman named Joseph Pujol, better known as "Le Petomane," stupefied and delighted Parisian society during his years at the Moulin Rouge (Red Windmill) with his ability to fart an amazing variety of sounds, including a yelping pup, his mother-in-law, and several musical instruments. Not only did he blow out a candle with his ass from a foot away; Le Petomane accompanied an orchestra, farting well-modulated notes, on key, in the appropriate spots. During Le Petomane's symphonies, the term "wind section" took on a new meaning.

Le Petomane alternately billed himself as "The Man with the Musical Derriere" and "The Only Artist Who Pays No Royalties." His specialty wasn't exactly new. At the beginning of the fifth century, Saint Augustine observed in *The City of God*, a chronicle of Rome's history, that "Some have such command of their bowels, that they can break wind continuously at pleasure, so as to produce the effect of singing"; French essayist Michel de Montaigne, referring to Augustine's example, wrote in 1580 that "[Joannes] Vives in his glosses [to *The City of God*] goes one better with a contemporary example of a [German in Maximilian's court] who could arrange to fart in tune with verses recited to him"; and for centuries Hindu yogis have trained themselves to use their sphincters to suck water into their rectums for ritual cleanings, expel it, then dry themselves by doing the same with air. But Le Petomane was the first Westerner to package this distinctive talent for mass consumption, as it were, and thus he became the most acclaimed farter of modern times.

(Apparently there have been many professional Japanese farters, called *misemono*, over the past several centuries. The shogun of shit-gassers was Kirifuri-hanasaki-otoko—"the mist-descending flower-blossom man"—who performed at the Ryogoku Bridge in Edo, now Tokyo, in 1774, performing various drum patterns, the musical scale, fireworks, barking dogs, and crowing roosters with his asshole. His *pièce de résistance* was a cartwheel accompanied by farting sounds resembling a water mill. There is also reported to be a modern *misemono* who, in the early 1980s, farted a tune along with an orchestra and then fired darts from a blowgun in his ass on an afternoon TV show.)

According to Le Petomane's French biographers, Jean Nohain and F. Caradec, he was a fixture in Parisian music halls between 1892 and 1900. At a time when actress Sarah Bernhardt could expect to draw 8,000 francs in box office receipts in one day, Le Petomane brought in 20,000 francs worth of business—easily outgrossing her in every way. Vocalist Yvette Guilbert, a contemporary of Le Petomane, recalled in her memoirs that one day Mr. Zidler, the manager of the Moulin Rouge, was visited by a pallid-faced man who told him, "I have a breathing arsehole. . . . I can open and shut it at will." According to Guilbert, Pujol requested a large basin filled with mineral water. He took off his trousers, sat himself in the basin, emptied it by sucking all the water into his bowels, then refilled it— leaving a slight scent of sulfur in the room.

At that point Pujol announced, "I can expel an almost infinite quantity of odourless gas."

"You're telling me you can fart," Zidler replied.

"Yes," Pujol said. But he could also "sing" through his asshole. To demonstrate, he provided his listener with a tenor, a baritone, a bass, the lead vocalist, and as an encore, "the mother-in-law." It was the mother-in-law that won Zidler over. He booked Pujol, now billed as Le Petomane, into the garden stage of the Moulin Rouge every evening from eight to nine. The *fartiste* was a hit on the first night. One observer noted that "laughter, shouting, women's shrieking and the whole hysterical din could be heard a hundred yards away from the Moulin Rouge."

The Moulin Rouge was an internationally popular music hall complex near the Place Pigalle in the bohemian Montmartre District. It consisted of a theater, where the infamous high-kicking cancan dancers were so airily captured by painter Toulouse-Lautrec, and a garden fronted by a large windmill—"a marvelous fan for my act," Le Petomane would later remark. The garden stage from which Le Petomane shook Paris was called the Elephant, because a colossal statue of an elephant dominated one side of it. Customers sat in the open air, at tables in wrought-iron chairs.

Le Petomane was a tall man with a bushy black mustache and closely cropped hair. Onstage he wore white gloves, a red coat, black satin pants with a little flap on the back, stockings, and patent leather shoes. During his act he remained straight-faced, and perhaps it was the incongruity of this deadly serious guy farting through the trapdoor in his pants that sent customers into spasms of laughter. "Women, stuffed in their corsets, were being carried out by nurses," one observer wrote.

Joseph Pujol was born in Marseilles on June 1, 1857, the first child of a stonemason. After several teenage years of apprenticing as a baker, he opened his own shop on a street that would later bear his last name. In 1883 he married a butcher's daughter and began producing the first of his ten children. He seemed like a solid citizen.

But one day, while he was fulfilling his military service, he told a couple of his regimental buddies that as a boy he had experienced an extraordinary event. Swimming along one of Marseilles's beaches, he dove underwater and held his breath. Suddenly he felt something cold seep deep into his stomach. As he ran out of the water and onto the beach, water poured out of his ass. He had never understood what happened, he said, and he hadn't gone back into the water since then. At the urging of the other soldiers, who were amused by the story, Pujol returned to the beach during leave to see if he could do it again. He discovered that with a little contraction of his abdominal muscles, he could suck as much water as he wanted into his lower bowels. Back at camp, he began to entertain his friends by sitting in water basins and emptying them, then squirting water from his ass. From water he moved to air. By holding his breath he could vacuum air into his ass, then force it back out with as much gusto and modulation as he wished, depending on how tightly he contracted his sphincter.

After his discharge, Joseph Pujol returned to his bakery in Marseilles and amused his friends and customers on the side. Eventually a local promoter persuaded him to try his luck as a performer. The man leased a hall and announced the upcoming show on posters and handbills all around the city. By now Pujol had decided upon a title for himself, the rather formal and respectable Le Petomane (the farting man), after discarding the crasser sobriquet Le Peteur (the farter). After the first few shows, there was no further need to advertise. The hall was packed every night. From Marseilles, Pujol took his act on the road into the nearby provinces. One newspaper writer in Toulon had this to say about the performance:

> At the beginning of the show, facing the audience, he explained that he had the power of breathing in air by the anus, just as we normally breathe in by the mouth. Then by means of this body of air contained in his intestines, he could at will produce all sorts of sounds.
>
> Then turning his back on the public, he announced the kind of noise he was going to make. I remember having heard the mason's round fart, the timid little fart of the young girl, etc.
>
> The seance ended with an attempt to run through the gamut of sounds. In reality he produced only four notes, the do, mi, sol, and do of the octave. I cannot guarantee that each of these notes was tonally true.

Through his early performances Pujol cherished one dream: to play at the Moulin Rouge. Finally, after tightening up his act, he felt like he was ready to take the plunge. The year was 1892. The rest is history.

Louis Pujol, who later worked onstage with his father, recalled Le Petomane's Moulin Rouge act in his memoirs: "Ladies and gentlemen," Le Petomane would announce to his audience, "I have the honor to present a session of Petomanie. The word *Petomanie* means someone who can break wind at will, but don't let your nose worry you. My parents ruined themselves scenting my rectum." Then he began a series of lightweight farts. "This one is a little girl, this the mother-in-law, this the bride on her wedding night [very quiet] and the morning after [very loud], this the mason [dry—no cement], this the dressmaker tearing two yards of calico [he let one rip for about ten seconds]." He completed this part of the performance with the booming of a cannon.

"Then my father would disappear for a moment behind the scenes to insert the end of a rubber tube, such as are used for enemas," Louis Pujol wrote. "It was about a yard long and he would take the other end in his fingers and in it place a cigarette as if it were in his mouth." Le Petomane puffed on the cigarette with his sphincter, removed the tube and blew smoke out his ass. Then he inserted a little flute and played a couple of tunes. As an encore he extinguished several gas flames and invited the audience to sing along with him.

An article in the May 1, 1894, edition of *Le Petit Journal* described Le Petomane as "a more or less lyrical artist whose melodies, songs without words, do not come exactly from the heart. To do him justice it must be said that he has pioneered something entirely his own, warbling from the depth of his pants those trills which others, their eyes toward heaven, beam at the ceiling." Eugene Forrier, writing for *Gil Blas Illustre*, commented, "With plenty of tact he knows exactly the right note to strike, discreet in society, matey with the bourgeoisie, serious with politicians and with the common herd he goes flat out, even does it to excess. He knows his public."

Le Petomane was such a hit in Paris that he was able to move his family into a chalet and ease their lives with servants. His contract with the Moulin Rouge also allowed him to slip away from the city on brief tours now and then and go where the winds blew him: several times into Belgium, where King Leopold II was an enthusiastic fan, and at least once to North Africa. In Madrid his act was considered so scandalous that authorities forced him to complete his commitments working as a clown, without farting.

Le Petomane became the willing subject of several well-regarded scientific inquiries. In 1892 he was written up in at least two major medical journals. In the more detailed investigation, Dr. Marcel Baudouin, writing in *La Semaine Medicale*, explained that his first concern was whether Le Petomane's farting was a physical curiosity or simply a parlor trick. Pujol himself agreed to be tested at

the Practical School of the Faculty of Medicine in Paris under the
observations of two doctors from the anatomy department. "Under
these conditions," wrote Baudouin, "it was easy to ensure that there
was nothing supernatural or artificial."

Le Petomane, Baudouin observed,

> has a physique in which nothing is exaggerated, except for cer-
> tain muscles—those which he exercises most frequently in his
> somewhat unusual profession—and is in first rate condition. . . .
>
> In a state of repose the anus shows no sign of abnormality
> but is perhaps a little more dilated than is usual. The sphincter
> is strong and elastic. There are no hemorrhoids in spite of the
> muscular work which takes place in this region every day, as
> we shall see. The rectum too is normal and does not seem
> dilated.

In the laboratory, Pujol bent over until his upper body was
horizontal. "Then he grips with his hands the top part of his knees
on both sides thus giving a solid support to his upper body," wrote
Baudouin.

> He then takes a very little breath and stiffens his arms. . . .
> There are obvious signs of real and intense strain, which are
> very easy to observe if the subject is undressed and the exhibi-
> tion is not taking place in public.
>
> After a few moments and following muscular efforts which
> are difficult to analyze, the digestive tube is completely filled
> with as much air as it can contain under such conditions. The
> subject then gently stands up almost vertical. The reservoir is
> full and can so remain for a certain time but not for long.
> Little by little it empties itself of its own accord unnoticed if
> Le Petomane does not force the air out himself.
>
> The amusing part of this exercise constitutes the second
> part of the phenomenon—the forcing out of the air accumu-
> lated in the intestine, acting as a reservoir, the breathing out.

By expelling this air, either standing upright, leaning forward, or bent double, and by a thousand different ways dependent on the state of contraction or relaxation of the anal sphincter on the one hand and of the muscles controlling the variation in capacity of the abdominal cavity on the other, Le Petomane can obtain effects which are both as brilliant as they are surprising and unforeseen.

When the gas comes out with enough force and with a certain degree of tension from the sphincter, noises are produced of intensity, timbre and of great variety. At times these are genuinely musical sounds. Although as it is almost impossible to obtain given notes, these turn out to be common chords or, what is more extraordinary, recognizable tunes. Le Petomane imitates all sorts of sounds such as the violin, the bass and the trombone. He can produce a strong enough note ten or twelve times running and he can take in enough air to produce sound lasting ten or fifteen seconds.

Without clothes the subject can extinguish a candle at a distance of twelve inches by the force of gas violently expelled from the anus. As this is air which has only been a few moments in the intestine there is no smell such as there would be from gases of intestinal origin.

Several years later, another scientific investigator, Dr. Adrien Charpy, noted that Pujol's main instruments were his abdominal muscles. He observed in 1904 that

Le Petomane uses his abdominal cavity like a bellows, the anterior and posterior walls being the two valves, the rectum the pipe. He inspires and expires. Crouched in a position which makes breathing difficult, he forces the anterior wall of the stomach against the posterior wall, and as he takes up this first position, a void is caused in the large intestine, air or water fills this through the open anus and the bellows are charged.

In reverse the muscular wall presses down on the full colon
and causes it to expel air or water.

By 1894, Le Petomane felt that he should be making more
money. Also, the Moulin Rouge had angered him by threatening a
lawsuit after he displayed part of his act as a favor to a friend at a
nearby farmers' market. So he broke his contract and built his own
portable traveling show, called Theatre Pompadour. "Maybe I'll fart
less loudly," he said, admitting that he'd miss the promotion and
prestige of the Moulin Rouge, "but I shall be free." The music hall
sued him for 3,000 francs and won. *Le Petit Journal* facetiously
noted: "When the Director of the Moulin Rouge heard of [Pujol's
violation of contract], he had the idea of going after him and bringing him back with some well placed kicks in . . . his musical area;
but on reflection and not wishing to damage the instrument, he has
preferred the law to stick its nose into this affair."

Pujol exacted revenge when he found out that the Moulin
Rouge had replaced him with a *farteuse* named Angele Thiebeau,
working under the name La Femme Petomane. It turned out that
she was just a blowhard, a *faux fartiste* who employed a bellows
hidden beneath her skirt. Pujol sued the Moulin Rouge, but before
his case reached the courtroom Mademoiselle Thiebeau put herself
out of business by unsuccessfully suing a local magazine for calling
her act "a practical joke in bad taste." The unfavorable publicity
ended the matter. (There was also a comic at the time who imitated
Le Petomane under the name Le Ventomane; the punch line of his
act was that he accidentally shit himself and ran terror-stricken
from the stage.)

Now topping his own variety-house bill, Le Petomane
expanded his act to include the sounds of animals and birds. He also
brought several of his children into the show. In time his act became
less renowned, but Pujol maintained a steady career until the World
War intruded in 1914 and took away all four of his sons. After the
armistice, when gas attacks no longer seemed humorous to the bat-
tered French, he gave up his act altogether and applied himself to
building several bakeries in Marseilles and a biscuit factory in
Toulon (where he may have floated a few biscuits of his own).

Joseph Pujol, Le Petomane, died in Toulon in 1945, at the age of eighty-eight. A medical school offered 25,000 francs for the right to examine his body, but his children declined.

Since then, Le Petomane has become the stuff of legend. His story became a comic strip in a 1975 issue of *Apple Pie* magazine and the better part of a 1976 comic book called *The Compleat Fart*, both of which featured him farting on the cover. In the 1980s, writer-character actor Timothy Carey, with assistance from painter Salvador Dali, invoked the figure and the "let-it-all-out" conscious-ness of Le Petomane during a murder trial (a man accidentally killed a woman when he farted) in a bizarre stage play called *The Insect Trainer*, subtitled *Le Pet*. While casting the play, Carey told *Filmfax* magazine, "I'd take a big fart in front of [the actors]. That's always a big help. I always thought if you really want to be a good actor, you've got to be able to fart in public."

An American comedy juggling quartet called the Flying Karamazov Brothers—Paul Magid, Howard Jay Patterson, Michael Preston, and Sam Williams—tried to resurrect the famed French farter in a play called *Le Petomane: A Comedy of Airs*.

According to Patterson, who played the lead, he strapped two small tanks of CO_2 under his clothes, released gas through a kind of whoopee whistle by activating the tank valves with a trigger bar on his waist, and controlled the pitch with a choke attached to his fingers. "We wanted to present Pujol as part of the French avant-garde of that time," says Patterson, "but most people didn't look past the farting." After running briefly in 1992 at the famed La Jolla Playhouse near San Diego, the piece was beefed up for a major mounting two years later in Texas at the Dallas Theater Center. Unfortunately, as soon as the board members of the well-endowed theater got wind of the subject matter, they nixed it.

The following year, 1995, turned out to be a watershed. TV actor Kelsey Grammer, star of the NBC comedy *Frazier*, confided to Jay Leno on the *Tonight Show* that he'd been developing a flatulent character named Mr. Methane, based on Le Petomane, for a one-man play (In fact, there is a Mr. Methane performing in England.) Meanwhile, another modern-day Le Petomane character, played by French actor Gerard Darmon, appeared as an itinerant performer in director Bigas Luna's Spanish film *Tit and the Moon*. Also that year, film actor Johnny Depp admitted that he pined to portray the legendary fart man. "You have to admire anyone with such great control of his . . . instrument," Depp told *Playboy*. "I'd love to play him. I'm sure there were tragic moments in his life. It's tragic that he left no successors. . . . That's a role I'd do in a minute."

In fact successors do exist and are farting proudly. Paul Oldfield, an Englishman in his early thirties, has been performing under the name Mr. Methane for the past decade or so. Capable of farting in three different tones, he accompanies rock and classical tunes, recites Shakespeare with pooting punctuations, blows talcum-powder plumes and blue darters across the stage, and extinguishes candles—all while costumed in a green outfit with a purple *M* on his chest. Mr. Methane's most memorable performance to date was farting the British national anthem on Swedish television. You can contact him through his Web page, www.mrmethane.com. In America, there is also a flesh-and-blood Le Petomane legacy. On Howard Stern's nationwide radio show on June 19, 1998, four American farters gathered on-air for Stern's First Annual Crepitation Contest. Three of them used the Pujol technique of sucking air into their assholes and then blowing it back out again with sustained, controlled bursts. (The fourth, a young woman, let what she called old-fashioned "log-filtered" farts.) Two weeks later, on July 2—a historic date among fart lovers—Stern ushered three of his fartists, including the attractive *farteuse*, onto Earvin "Magic" Johnson's short-lived Fox-TV talk show, *The Magic Hour*, in order to showcase their flatal talents accompanying the 1963 surf tune, "Wipe Out." Magic Johnson's ratings more than doubled overnight, as a proud nation held its breath and the ghost of Joseph Pujol looked down.

But wait, two months later, on August 26, 1998, a 15-year-old kid visiting *The Howard Stern Show* pushed the envelope even further by cracking off 400 farts in less than two hours. Stern aired part of this demonstration three days later on his Saturday night CBS TV show.

Damn, *that's* entertainment!

UH-OH, HE SHIT HIS PANTS!

This guy's got a singing asshole, see. He goes into a swanky club and tells the owner his anus can sing as sweetly as Elvis or k. d. lang. When the proprietor offers him a spot in the show, he steps onstage, takes the microphone, makes a big production of warming up, and—boom—lets a tremendous fart that knocks over everybody's drinks. The punch line is "Excuse me, I had to clear my throat."

This has been a popular joke over the years because the guy proudly show-cases his intestinal gas in public. If anybody's uncomfortable, it's the audience, not him. A primitive part of us—that inner toddler who once delighted in farting and shitting in our diapers—finds such vainglorious venting admirable. Here's a similar joke:

A grade school teacher asks her pupils to make up a sentence using the word definitely.

Little Brittany's hand goes up. "Miss Bango, the sky is definitely blue."

"Not always," Miss Bango corrects her. "Sometimes the sky is red, or gray, or even yellow."

Kimberly's hand shoots up. "Teacher, teacher, the grass is definitely green."

Miss Bango shakes her head. "Not always. Sometimes the grass is yellow or brown."

The class falls silent. Little Ray cautiously stands up with a quizzical look on his face. "Miss Bango, when you fart, is there supposed to be a lump in it?"

Since the boy seems sincere, she answers, "No, I don't believe so, Ray."

"Well, in that case, Miss Bango, I have definitely shit in my pants!"

In yet another joke, a wet farter turns his mishap to someone else's disadvantage: Johnny and Bobby are sitting on opposite ends of Bobby's bed trying to fart during a game of "bed football." Each fart is a touchdown worth six points, and Bobby's leading eighteen to six. Johnny is staging a comeback when, suddenly, he accidentally shits himself.

Bobby looks at the stinky mess on Johnny's end of the bed and shakes his head, "Uh-oh, what'll we do now?"

"It's half-time," Johnny announces. "Now we change sides."

In most fart jokes, however, the farters are shamed and we feel embarrassed for them. The most well known of these, and the longest, is the "Crepitation Contest," detailed in chapter 9.

For a nice twist on the theme, here's one about a man who gets on a crowded bus and spots an empty aisle seat next to an elderly lady. As he sits down, he accidentally blasts off a fart. Embarrassed but feigning innocence and nonchalance, he asks the lady, "Excuse me, ma'am, do you have today's paper?"

"No," she says, "but when we pass the next tree, I'll reach out and grab a handful of leaves."

Here's yet another variation. Millie's sick of the way her husband farts in his sleep every night. Her complaints that it sounds like he's blowing his guts out have no effect on him. So finally she decides to teach him a lesson. At the supermarket she buys some chicken gizzards. While her husband is sleeping she arranges them on the bed under his ass. A half hour later she's fixing breakfast when he comes into the kitchen and says, "Well, honey, you were right. I farted my guts out. But don't worry, I managed to stuff them all back inside again!"

5

LIT. FARTS

And my flatterers shall be the pure and gravest
of divines that I can get for money. My mere
fools eloquent burgesses, and then my poets,
the same that writ so subtly of the fart, whom
I will entertain still for that subject.

—Ben Jonson, The Alchemist *(1610)*

The guardians of decency would have us believe that the written fart can be found only in the works of perverted hacks and dirty old scribes (like myself) morbidly fixated on their bowel movements. Don't believe 'em. Some of the world's greatest literary giants have found fun, frolic, folly, tomfoolery, and a joyful noise with flatulence, and naturally I'm proud to cram their hallowed names into my book in order to spiff up the index and make this whole sordid enterprise look more impressive than it really is.

Greece's illustrious Old Comedian, Aristophanes, was introduced in chapter 1 with an observation about fart humor in a scene from *Frogs*, but his greatest tributes to flatulence occur in one of his most popular works, *The Clouds*, written in 423 B.C. Early in the play a student recounts Socrates's lecture on the farts of gnats: "He explained that the guts of a gnat are hollow, a sort of narrow tube," says the student. "The air is sucked in at the front, and forced under pressure down and out the back. It's the narrowness of the hole that makes the noise."

"It's a kind of trumpet, then, a gnat's behind?" his friend

Strepsiades asks. "What a brilliant man he must be, what an expert on a gnat's anatomy!"

Much later in *The Clouds* we find Socrates trying to explain thunder to Strepsiades and ascribing it to "Dinos—The Great Wind." "I said the clouds were full of water, didn't I, jostling, crowding along? That's what makes them rumbling. . . . All right. Think about yourself. You know that stew you always buy at festivals? You stuff yourself with that, and right away it sloshes and gurgles round your guts inside."

"Apollo, yes! My belly starts to churn, and boils and rumbles," says Strepsiades. "Quietly at first . . . pa-pax, *pa-pax* . . . then a bit louder . . . *pa-pa*-pax! And it always ends with a real eruption . . . *pa-pa-pa-pax! pa-pa-pax!* Thunder, just like them."

"You see?" Socrates says. "If your little crap makes all that noise, just think of the thunder the sky can make."

Horace, the great Roman poet, included a tale (number eight) in his first *Satire* (circa 34 B.C.), "The Hag Canidia—As Observed by Priapus," that presented the fart as a scatterer of evil. Horace wrote in the voice of the god Priapus, who was hewn into a scarecrow from the trunk of a wild fig tree, to guard the public cemetery at Esquiline from grave robbers and jackals. But because he's simply "a useless log," he can't frighten off the two witches, Canidia and Sagana, who are "gathering bones and noxious herbs under the waning moon's fair face." The hags rip the earth of the graveyard with their fingernails, tear a lamb to pieces and poor the blood into a ditch, and call upon the gods of the underworld. "You could see snakes and hell-hounds straggling about," wrote Horace, "while the shamefaced moon hid behind the great tombs in order not to look upon such doings."

But not to worry, for the fart will come to the rescue. "I was a witness not incapable of revenge," Horace wrote, "for, with the sound of a bursting bladder, my fig-tree buttocks popped and split. Off [the witches] scampered to the city. You would have had no end of fun seeing Canidia lose her false teeth, and Sagana her tall wig, and watching the herbs and the charmed bracelets drop from their arms."

Probably the first English language masterpiece, written in

Middle English verse, was Geoffrey Chaucer's *Canterbury Tales*, a literary pilgrimage that he worked on for more than a dozen years, probably between 1386 and 1399, and died before completing. The *Canterbury Tales* was the chronicle of—and a collection of fables as told by—a group of sojourners on their way to Canterbury Cathedral, where the sacred bones of St. Thomas à Beckett are enshrined. Chaucer provided two of his tales with flatulent punch lines, and both have reverberated over the centuries with the gusto of a good church fart.

To summarize the tales, I have blended the texts of both Chaucer's original Middle English and a modern translation by R. M. Lumiansky. One of the more popular of the stories is "The Miller's Tale," which according to Professor Thomas W. Ross contains "the most famous lover's rebuke in literature." The spurned suitor was a parish clerk named Absolon, described by Chaucer as a fastidious young dandy who was squeamish about breaking wind ("*somdeel squaymous of fartying*"). In the dead of a moonless night he comes to the window of Alison, a young married woman he's had his eye on, to plead his love. But Alison, who is already in the midst of an adulterous affair with another man, has no use for Absolon. "Go forth thy way, or I wol cast a ston," she threatens.

"Than kiss me," Absolon begs from outside her window.

"Woltou than go thy way therewith?" she asks.

"Ye, certainly, sweetheart."

"Than make thee ready. I come anon." When she opened her window and swung her hairy buttocks out the window, Absolon "kist hir naked ers." Immediately he "thought it was amiss for well he wist a woman hath no beerd." Alison laughed and slammed the window shut.

Angry at love and swearing revenge, Absolon goes across the street to the blacksmith, who's working late, and borrows a branding iron from the furnace. He returns to Alison's window with the white-hot poker in his hand and tells her he has brought her a golden ring to exchange for another kiss. Alison's boyfriend, Nicholas, having already arisen from bed "for to pisse," decides that he'll put a finishing touch on the joke. He opens the window and proffers his own hairy ass for a kiss. "Spek, sweete bryd, I noot not where thou art," Absolon says, whereupon "this Nicholas anon leet fle a fart, as greet as it had been a thonder-dent" in his face. Absolon promptly jams the hot iron "amid the ers" of poor Nicholas, whose shrieks of pain begin a comical series of events too complicated to detail here.

In "The Summoner's Tale," greedy Friar John—the precursor of today's televangelist—goes from town to town and house to house, begging for contributions towards his friary's ministry of saving lost souls and the erection of a new church. Finally he comes to the home of a well-to-do but bedridden old man named Thomas. Determined to take Thomas and his family for everything they own, the friar makes himself at home and preaches to the old man about charity. He explains how the piety and self-imposed poverty of humble friars like himself magnify the power of their prayers in the eyes of God. When Thomas grumbles that these prayers, which always cost him a lot of money, have done him no good in the past, Friar John dodges the subject by quoting scripture about the evil of wrath.

By now old Thomas can't stand any more of this nonsense. "I shall give something to your holy convent while I am alive," he says, "and you shall have it in your hand at once, upon this condition and no other: that you so divide it, my dear brother, that every friar will have an equal share. This you must swear upon your faith, without fraud or cavil."

"I swear it," says Friar John, "by my faith."

"Now, then," Thomas continues, "put your hand down my back and grope around carefully. Beneath my buttocks you will find a thing which I secretly hid there." As the friar reaches under and gropes beneath the old man's asshole, Thomas breaks wind in the middle of his hand. ("*Amydde his hand he leet the frere a fart.*") "There is no nag drawing a cart that could have broken wind so loudly," Chaucer wrote.

The friar leaps away, cursing and shouting. "You shall regret this fart, if I can arrange it!"

When Friar John complains to the local lord, calling Thomas "a blasphemer who charged me to divide that which cannot be divided equally among all," the lord treats it as a mathematical problem: How can the "sound or savour of a fart" be divided into equal shares? The lord's squire, sitting nearby at the table, devises a solution. On a calm day, without wind, a cartwheel will be brought to the lord's manor house, along with the twelve other friars in John's order. They will kneel down at the end of each spoke and press their noses against them while the old gentleman farts into the axle. As for John, being the worthiest of his cloister, he'll get the first whiff by pressing his nose upright under the axle hole. And so the gift is equally distributed.

Chaucer also slipped in a couple of puns, first by having the friar ask Thomas for "ferthyngs" (which could be taken as either quarter-pennies or small farts) and by calling the division of Thomas's flatulence an "ars-metrike" problem, referring both to arithmetic and to an ass ("ars") measurement.

Two final Chaucer farts: In the prologue to "The Summoner's Tale," the summoner makes a quick joke about Satan pulling up his tail and farting 20,000 friars out of his asshole. In "The Pardoner's Tale," the pardoner (a cleric given the power to pardon sins, as long as the sinner could pay enough money) preaches about the evils of gluttony and even criticizes his own generous gut, filled with "dong" and corruption! "At either end of thee foul is the sound," he tells his companions. (For more on these scenes as interpreted cinematically by Italian director Pier Paolo Pasolini, see chapter 10.)

Chaucer's Italian counterpart was Dante Alighieri, a literary colossus who wrote the lengthy narrative poem *The Divine Comedy* over several years, almost right up to his death in 1321. It was composed of three separate sections: *The Inferno*, *Purgatory*, and *Paradise*, most of them written while Dante languished in political exile. Dante was, like Chaucer, a man of the world, a politician and statesman with a great insight into the human condition. He was also, like Chaucer, a man who loved the fables of his time and told them in the vernacular of common people.

The Inferno, the most popular book of *The Divine Comedy*, details Dante's visit through the circles of hell, guided by the Latin poet Virgil. In the eighth circle, Dante meets a group of tormented souls, condemned for the sin of flattery, who are fated to live out eternity in a river of shit "that seemed the overflow of the world's latrines." As Dante and Virgil prepare to find a bridge to the next area, they're given an escort of demons:

> They [demons] turned along the left bank in a line;
> but before they started, all of them together
> had stuck their pointed tongues out as a sign [razz]
> to their captain that they wished permission to pass,
> and he made a trumpet of his ass.
> (Canto XXI)

While still in the eighth circle, Dante and Virgil encounter several individuals who were damned for provoking marital discord and tearing asunder what God had meant to be united; as punishment their bodies have been hideously mutilated:

> A wine tun when a stave or cant-bar starts
> does not split open as wide as one I saw
> split from his chin to the mouth with which man farts.
> Between his legs all of his red guts hung
> with the heart, the lungs, the liver, the gall bladder,
> and the shriveled sac that passes shit to the bung.
> (Canto XXVIII)

Elizabethan playwright William Shakespeare is considered by many to be the English language's foremost literary titan. He never wrote "Hark! What wind through yonder buttocks breaks?" and his line "Ill blows the wind that profits nobody" (from *Henry VI, Part III*) has nothing to do with flatulence. But Shakespeare did show an occasional fondness for fart puns and imagery. For example, in act 3 of *A Comedy of Errors* (c. 1594), he couldn't resist playing with the various meanings of the term breaking wind: "A man may break a word with you, sir; and words are but wind; Ay, and break it in your face, so he break it not behind."

In *Hamlet* (c. 1601), where something was rotten in the state of Denmark, the Bard sneaked in the vulgar sound of a fart by invoking and punning upon the "buzzer"—the Elizabethan version of the razzberry—familiar to any ham actor who'd ever aroused an audience's scorn. In act 2, as a theatrical troupe arrives to reenact the murder of his father, Hamlet is having the following exchange with his father's old friend, Polonius:

HAMLET: My lord, I have news to tell you. When Roscius was an actor in Rome,—
POLONIUS: The actors are come hither, my lord.
HAMLET: *Buz, buz!*
POLONIUS: Upon my honor,—
HAMLET: Then came each actor on his ass,—

Shakespeare's friend Ben Jonson likewise punned on the word *buzz* in his masque play *Oberon, The Fairy Prince* (1611), when a gaggle of satyrs chants:

Buzz, quoth the blue fly,
Hum, quoth the bee;
Buzz and hum they cry,
And so do we.
In his ear, in his nose,
Thus, do you see?

Shakespeare used flatulent metaphor in *Henry IV, Part I* (c. 1597), when Hotspur observes in act 3, "Diseased nature oftentimes breaks forth/ In strange eruptions; Oft the teaming earth/ Is with a kind of colic pinch'd and vex'd/ By the imprisoning of unruly wind/ Within her womb."

Witches were traditionally plagued by deadly odors and poisonous vapors, thanks to their diet of onions, cabbages, and any number of nocturnal herbs, not to mention their melancholic temperaments; and demonology credited them with the ability to raise storms and tempests. So it seems only natural that in act 1 of *Macbeth* (c. 1606) the three witches of "toil and trouble . . . Fire burn and cauldron bubble" infamy are nearly farting at each other with puns while they conjure up a gale or two:

SECOND WITCH: "I'll give thee wind—"
FIRST WITCH: "Thou 'rt kind.—"

THIRD WITCH: "And I another."
FIRST WITCH: "I myself have all the other, and the very ports they blow, all the quarters that they know."

And in act 5 of *Much Ado About Nothing* (c. 1598) the swain Benedick is taken aback when he tries to kiss Beatrice. She scolds him, "Foul words is but foul wind, and foul/ Wind is foul breath, and foul breath is noisome;/ Therefore I will depart unkissed." Does that sound like an early case of fart breath?

In act 3 of *Othello* (c. 1604) a couple of puns await the dedicated fart watcher:

CLOWN: Are these, I pray you, wind-instruments?
FIRST MUSICIAN: Ay, marry, are they, sir.
CLOWN: O, thereby hangs a tail.
FIRST MUSICIAN: Why hangs a tale, sir?
CLOWN: Marry, sir, by many a wind-instrument that I know.

Finally, though this may be stretching it a bit, a servant in act 4 of *Coriolanus* (c. 1608) seems to be comparing the clatter of battle to greeting the morning with a loud yawn and a good fart: "[War] exceeds peace as far as day does night; it's sprightly, waking, audible, and full of vent."

Ben Jonson, Shakespeare's colleague at London's Globe Theatre, was also one of the era's most popular poets and playwrights. But whereas Shakespeare wrote mostly of history and fantasy, Jonson delighted in telling contemporary stories in what would now be called the language of the streets. One finds in his work, for example, that *punk* was an early word for prostitute.

Jonson began act 4 of *Epicene*, or *A Silent Woman* (1609), one of his comedies, with the description of a clamorous young bride, Epicene, at a mock wedding: "The spitting, the coughing, the laughter, the neezing, the farting, dancing, noise of the music, and her masculine and loud commanding, and urging the whole family, makes him think he has married a furie." The "husband" himself, Morose by name, laments later, "You do not know in what a misery I have been exercised this day, what a torrent of evil! My very house turns round with the tumult! I dwell in a windmill." The "wife," incidentally, turns out to be a young man in drag.

Several times during his career, Ben Jonson wrote what were called masques—extravagantly costumed entertainments sponsored by wealthy or royal patrons for private viewings. One of them, *The Gypsies Metamorphosed*, was commissioned in 1621 by George Villiers, the earl of Buckingham, for a secret, out-of-the-way party being given for King James, the earl's homosexual lover. Within the masque play is a ballad about Cock Lorel, a legendary gypsy rogue who, according to Jonson, invited Satan to dinner at a real-life limestone cave in the Derbyshire hills called the Devil's Arse. Known also as Peak's Hole or Peac's Arse, the half-mile-deep cave was long famous not only for being a gypsy hangout but also for the strong winds that blew from its bowels.

In Jonson's "Ballad of Cock Lorel" the gypsy assumes the role of master chef for the devil in order to serve him various members of what was then London's middle class, all of whom would later be blasted away in a fart that gave the Devil's Arse its name:

> Cock Lorel would needs have the devil his guest,
> And bade him once into the Peak to dinner,
> Where never the fiend had such a feast
> Provided him yet at the charge of a sinner.
> His stomach was queasy for coming there coached;
> The jogging had caused some crudities rise;
> To help it he called for a Puritan poached,
> That used to turn up the eggs of his eyes.

Then the devil begins to eat a "promoter in plum broth . . . Six pickled tailors sliced and cut," a "rich fat usurer stewed in his marrow, and by him a lawyer's head and green sauce, both which his belly took in like a barrow." Also on the menu was "a cloven sergeant's face; the sauce was made of his yeoman's brains that had been beaten out with his own mace." There were two roasted sheriffs, then "the very next dish was the mayor of a town" with "his couple of hench-boys boiled to a jelly."

The list of hapless Londoners goes on and on, until:

All which devoured, he then for a close
Did for a full draught of Darby [ale] call;
He heaved the huge vessel up to his nose,
And left not till he had drunk up all.
Then from the table he gave a start,
Where banquet and win were nothing scarce,
All which he flirted [flicked] away with a fart,
From whence it was called the Devil's Arse.
And there he made such a breech with the wind,
The hole too standing open the while,
That the scent of the vapor before and behind
Hath foully perfumed most part of the isle.

By way of the devil's guts, Ben Jonson handily turned many of his overfed countrymen into gas and then blew them away with a rip-snorter. He even said that England smells like shit; and he said it in front of England's king.

Finally, in his poem "Epigram 133: On the Famous Voyage" (1616), Jonson wrote,

By this time had they reach'd the Stygian poole,
By which the Masters swear, when on the stoole [toilet]
Of worship, they their nodding chinnes doe hit
Against their breasts. Here, sev'rall ghosts did flit
About the shore, of farts, but late departed,
White, black, blew, greene, and in more formes out-started,
Then all those *Atomi* [atoms] ridiculous,
Whereof old *Democrite*, and *Hill Nicholas*,
One said, the other swore, the world consists.
These be the causes of those thicke frequent mists
Arising in that place, through which, who goes,
Must trie the un-used valor of a nose.

A contemporary of Shakespeare and Jonson was poet Sir John Davies, best known for resurrecting the Latin epigram form.

Around 1595, when he was a young man perfecting his craft, Davies wrote "In Leucam," describing the discombobulating effect a fart could have on a lady of delicate manner:

> Leuca in presence once a fart did let
> Some laughed a little; she forsook the place
> And, mad with shame, did her glove forget
> Which she returned to fetch with bashful grace
> And when she should have said, "This is my glove,"
> "My fart," quoth she, which did more laughter move.

(The embarrassment of a prim but flatulent lady carried on nearly 400 years later in John Barth's 1969 novel *The Floating Opera*. On a muggy July day, a secretary named Mrs. Lake, "a model of decorum," bent down to pick up her handkerchief "and most undaintily—oh, most indecorously—broke wind, virtually in my coffee." She blushed and fled the office, but the stench "hung heavy in the humid air, long past the lady's flight. It hung, it lolled, it wisped.")

Another of England's literary titans was William Blake, a visionary poet, illustrator, and early New Age spiritualist who's probably best known for the line "Tyger! Tyger! burning bright." A London Cockney, Blake wrote two poems that for flatulence lovers still burn as brightly as a lighted bean fart. The first is "Let the Brothels of Paris Be Opened," also known as "Lafayette" (1793), an adjunct to his earlier, lengthier poem *The French Revolution*.

> Let the Brothels of Paris be opened
> With many an alluring dance
> To awake the physicians thro the city
> Said the beautiful Queen of France [Marie Antoinette]
> Then old Nobodaddy [Old Daddy Nobody, King Louis XVI]
>   aloft
> Farted & belchd & coughd
> And said I love hanging & drawing & quartering
> Every bit as well as war & slaughtering

. . . .

The Queen of France just touched this Globe
And the Pestilence darted from her robe

Several years later Blake wrote "When Klopstock England Defied" (c. 1800) in which he mocked the ancient Egyptian idea, popularized in Blake's time by the German poet Friedrich Klopstock, that since man's body is a microcosm of a nature in which all things are unified, its inner workings are influenced by and influential upon all other things. If that were so, Blake joked, he could sit on the toilet in England and tamper with Klopstock's bowel movements in Germany:

When Klopstock England defied
Uprose terrible Blake in his pride
For old Nobodaddy [God] aloft
Farted & Belchd & coughd

. . . .

Blake was giving his body ease
At Lambeth beneath the poplar trees
From his seat then started he
And turnd himself round three times three
The Moon at that sight blushd scarlet red
The stars threw down their cups & fled
And all the devils that were in hell
Answered with a ninefold yell
Klopstock felt the intripled turn
And all his bowels began to churn
And his bowels turned round three times three
And lockd in his soul with a ninefold key
That from his body it neer could be parted
Till to the last trumpet it was farted

. . . .

If Blake could do this when he rose up from shite [shitting]
What might he not do if he sat down to write

Incidentally, Blake's popular poem "I Feared the Fury of My Wind" is not about farting—at least I don't think so, anyway.

The French have always loved a good fart (whereas their neighbors, the Germans, seem traditionally more obsessed with shit). Where else but Paris could a man build a theatrical career on his farting ability? No wonder France's greatest writers had something to say about passing gas.

One of the earliest was François Rabelais, a sixteenth-century Benedictine monk, physician, medical scholar, and parodist. Rabelais's lampoons and tall stories inspired a number of future satirists, including Jonathan Swift, Mark Twain, and Honoré de Balzac. His most famous book, *Gargantua and Pantagruel* (1532–62), follows the adventures of a vastly oversized father and son through Medieval Europe.

Gargantua is given to discoursing at length upon how to wipe his ass; he discovers that using a downy goose is the preferred method. As a boy he "bawled like a sick cow, hung his head and hid his face in his cap, and it was no more possible to draw a word from him than a fart from a dead donkey." He "grew . . . as full of matter as any goose liver ever crammed," and like any overfed student, "Gargantua dunged, piddled, vomited, belched, broke wind, yawned, pist, coughed, hiccoughed, sneezed and snotted himself as majestically and bountifully as an archdeacon." At one point Rabelais sits him down at a table and lists all of the games Gargantua played, including "Nose to Breech" and "A Salvo of Farts." When Gargantua visits a Friar John (no relation to Friar John in Chaucer's "The Summoner's Tale"), the cleric asks him why a young woman's inner thighs are so cool. Answering his own question, Friar John tells Gargantua, "It is for three cases which make a place naturally cool: in the first place, because the water runs all round it; secondly, because it is shady, obscure, a dark place never lit by the sun; and thirdly, because it is continuously fanned by winds from the northern hole. . . . And heartily, too."

Gargantua's son, Pantagruel, is so gigantic that at one point an illness has to be treated by huge laxative pills, each containing several men, lowered into his stomach so that the workers can then flush out his digestive tract. In a spoof of the pre-Renaissance education of undigested classic and ecclesiastic literature, Pantagruel travels to Paris and peruses the library at St. Victor, where Rabelais lists an entire catalog of compelling but often ridiculous book titles, including *The Art of Farting Decently in Public* by Hardouin de Graetz, a theologian of Cologne; *Tartaret, On Methods of Shitting*; and *The Wind Dispeller of the Apothecaries*. He encounters two characters named (depending upon which translation you read) Lord Kissmyarse and Lord Suckfizzle, Lords Kissbreech and Suckfist (*fist* and *fizzle* were early English words for soft farts), or Lords Kissasse and Bunfondle.

Pantagruel's most impressively flatulent exploit takes place when "with the fart that he let, the earth trembled nine leagues about, wherewith and with the corrupted air, he begot above three and fifty thousand little men, ill-favored dwarfs, and with one fisg [a small fart] that he let, he made as many little women." His friend Panurge asks, "How now are your farts so fertile and fruitful? By God, here be brave farted men, and fiqued women, let them be married together, they will beget fine hornets and dorflies."

In *The Hunchback of Notre Dame* (1831), novelist Victor Hugo illuminates an old French custom that concerned a fart. According to the nineteenth-century French playwright Victor Ducange, prostitutes who crossed a toll bridge at the village of Montluc near Paris in the fourteenth and fifteenth centuries were obliged to pay with a fart instead of the French equivalent of a farthing. This tradition may have come from the common medieval belief that Satan took a special interest in bridges. Hugo makes reference to the practice in the first chapter of his novel, when several derisive students celebrating Feast of the Fools Day in 1482 jeer a succession of passersby:

"Claude Choart! Dr. Claude Choart! Are you looking for Marie la Giffarde?"

"She's in the rue de Glatigny."

"She's making a bed for the king of the ribalds."

"She pays her four deniers—quattuor denarios."

"Aut unum bumbum." [Latin for "Or one fart."]

"Do you want her to pay you through the nose?"

In the early 1830s the novelist Honoré de Balzac wrote a

series of what his biographer André Maurois called "light-hearted tales of bawdry written in archaic language in the manner of Rabelais and other Touraine storytellers." This compendium came to be known as *Droll Stories*, and one of them, "The Jests of King Louis the Eleventh," may have been inspired by Suetonius's account of Emperor Claudius allowing farting at royal Roman banquets.

In Balzac's tale, King Louis loves to play tricks on the guests in his court. His wife, Nicole Beaupertuys, decides one day to amuse him and herself by making fools of several of these people, including a cardinal, a bishop, a judge, an envoy, and a captain of the Scottish guard. She tells the king "to make their guests drink hard and eat to repletion; that he was to make merry, and joke with them; but when the cloth was removed, he was to pick quarrels with them about trifles, dispute their words, and be sharp with them."

Inviting his guests to a "splendid and first-class supper," King Louis "stuffs them with green peas, returning to the hotch-potch, praising the plums, commending the fish, saying to one, 'Why do you not eat?,' to another, 'Drink to Madame'; to all of them, 'Gentlemen, taste these lobsters; put this bottle to death! . . . This game is my own hunting; he who takes it not offends me . . . Just give me your opinion of these preserves, they are Madame's own. Have some of these grapes, they are my own growing.'"

Soon the feast begins to nag at the revelers' innards. "Going into the salon again, they broke into a profuse sweat, began to blow, and to curse their gluttony. The king sat quietly apart; each of them was the more willing to be silent because all their forces were required for internal digestion of the huge platefuls confined in their stomachs, which began to wabble and rumble violently." Finally one of them, the cardinal, is compelled to belch loudly.

That's the king's cue to turn serious and rebuke his guests. "What does this mean, am I a simple clerk?" he demands, shocked that anyone would belch in his presence.

"This was heard with terror, because usually the king made much of a good belch well off the stomach. The other guests determined to get rid in another way of the vapours which were dodging about in their pancreatic retorts; and at first they endeavoured to hold them for a little while in the pleats of their mesenteries. It was then that some of them puffed and swelled like tax gatherers."

Meanwhile, the queen has put large dolls resembling another lady and herself on the only available toilets, so that if "they desire to mount the throne to which we are now about to pretend to go, they will always find the place taken; by this means you will enjoy their writhings."

The king goes from man to man, engaging each one in uncomfortable conversation. "All the guests were in a state of not knowing how to arrest the progress of the fecal matter to which nature has given, even more than to water, the property of finding a certain level. Their substances modified themselves and glided working downward, like those insects who demand to be let out of their cocoons, raging, tormenting, and ungrateful to the higher powers."

Unfortunately, since the toilets are taken and angry dogs have been positioned at the doors leading outside, the guests must struggle with their stuffed bowels and their urge to shit, fart, and piss without slighting or insulting the king. After all, "as these gentlemen were all nobodies, raised to their present position by the favour of the king, Louis, in a moment of anger, could crush them at will." The surgeon becomes "burdened with an accumulation which seriously impeded his private channels." The Scottish captain "tried gently to break wind, and spoiled his trousers. He went ashamed into a corner, hoping that before the king, his mishap might escape detection."

At the last moment the king laughs and lets them all go to the bathrooms. "The farce is good, but it is fetid," he says afterward.

In 1887 the French novelist Émile Zola introduced one of literature's most unabashed farters, a peasant named Jésus-Christ, in his earthy and rebellious tragedy *The Earth*. Zola was then in the middle of the French "naturalist" movement, recording the tiniest everyday details of common lives, so he spared no description of Jésus-Christ's farts and the way he used them. The following passage was one of several that led to Zola's British publisher being fined and imprisoned, despite the translator's expurgations of some of the nastier bits.

Jésus-Christ was a very windy fellow. Continual explosions blew through the house and livened things up. Damn it all, no one could ever be bored in that rascal's house, for he never let fly without blurting out some joke or other as well. He despised timid little squeaks, smothered between the cheeks, squirting out uneasily and ashamedly. He never emitted anything but frank detonation, substantial and ample as cannon shots. Whenever he raised his leg and settled himself with a comfortable and tactical motion, he called his daughter in tones of urgent command, with a grave expression on his face.

"La Trouille, hurry, for God's sake!"

She rushed up and the blast went off point blank with such a vibrating energy that she gave a jump.

"Run after it. Get hold of it between your teeth and see if there's any knots in it!"

At other times, as soon as she reached him he would give her his hand. "Pull hard, draggle-tail! Make it go off with a bang!"

At other times again, he raised an imaginary gun to his shoulder and took a long and careful sight; then after the shot was fired, he shouted, "Find it now, retrieve it, you lazy bitch!"

La Trouille choked and fell over on her backside with laughter. The joke never palled; in fact it was funnier every time.

Zola seems to have anticipated the arrival of Le Petomane, who would gain fame at the Moulin Rouge five years later, for he wrote of Jésus-Christ that "sometimes he had a whole posy of explosions, one for M. le Curé, one for le Maire, and another for the ladies. The fellow's belly, you'd have almost thought, was a music box from which he could extract any sound he liked; so much so that in the Jolly Ploughman at Cloyes they used to bet him: 'It's one on me if you let off six'; and he discharged six broadsides and won an overwhelming victory."

One evening at supper, as La Trouille brought a steaming dish of kidney beans to the table, "Jésus-Christ, before sitting down, let off three regular reports, full blast. 'Gun-salute for the feast! Now we can set to.' Then, bracing himself, he achieved a fourth, unique, tremendous and insulting. 'That's for those rotten Buteaus [his brother's family]. Hope it'll choke them!'"

A minute later, "Jésus-Christ, not wanting to let the conversation languish, let out a prolonged blast which went through the straw of his chair with the whining modulation of a human cry. He immediately turned to his daughter and solemnly inquired, 'What was that you said?'"

At the end of the meal,

Slowly Jésus-Christ tilted to one side, thundered, then looked at the door and shouted, "Come in!"

Old Fouan [his father] took up the challenge. He had been feeling out of things for some time now. He regained something of his youth, lifted his buttock, and thundered in turn, replying, "Here I come!"

The two men slapped each other's hands, slobbering and laughing cheek to cheek. They were enjoying themselves. The scene was altogether too magnificent for La Trouille, who had collapsed on the floor. So shaken was she with wild screams of laughter that she too let off an explosion—but a tiny one, soft and musical, like the thin note of a fife in comparison with the deep organ-notes of the two men.

Indignant and disgusted, Jésus-Christ rose and extended his arm in a gesture of tragic authority.

"Out of here, you filthy! Out of here, you stinkpot! By God, I'll teach you to show respect for your father and grandfather."

He had never allowed her such familiarity. The sport was reserved for grown-ups. He waved his hand in the air, pretending to be asphyxiated by the little flute-puff—his own, he said, smelt only of gunpowder.

Throwing her out of the room with a shove, he tells her, "You dirty lump, go out and shake your skirt! And don't return for an hour, not till you've been properly aired."

One of the world's most colossal literary assemblages is *The Arabian Nights*, a medieval Arabic manuscript of tales—gathered over several hundred years, up to about the fifteenth century—that have been traced back to ancient Indian, Persian, and Arabic cultures. Europe was introduced to this mammoth tome at the beginning of the eighteenth century, after Antoine Galland found a copy in Syria and had it sent home to Paris, where he translated it into French under the title *A Thousand Nights and One Night*. English versions, using the title *The Arabian Nights' Entertainments*, began to appear in the early 1800s. Probably the most extensive of them was translated from both Galland's French edition and an original Arabic manuscript by the noted explorer Richard Burton and published in 1885.

The Arabian Nights is a lengthy series of stories within stories, most of them told by a young fabulist named Scheherazade who must keep her bridegroom, the king, so enthralled by her yarns that he'll refrain from having her executed at dawn—the fate of all his previous brides. Probably the most familiar narratives within the work are the adventures of Aladdin, Sinbad, and Ali Baba and his forty thieves. Less well known is the story Scheherazade tells on her 410th night, called "How Abu Hasan Brake Wind," because after Burton included it in his version, subsequent editors, deeming the story unfit for children and other delicate folk, expurgated it from popular editions. Some scholars even claim that "How Abu Hasan Brake Wind" didn't exist in the original Arabic book, but rather was fabricated by Richard Burton himself. In any event, he's the only translator who included it.

"How Abu Hasan Brake Wind" is a joke told in fable, but it gives an idea of what low esteem a fart held among the Arab merchant class some thousand years ago, when the story takes place. A widower named Abu Hasan, having deserted the Bedouin life to live a more stable existence in the city, becomes a prosperous merchant and decides it's time to remarry. His wedding banquet is a major event. Everyone, "kith and kin . . . friends and foes and all his acquaintances of that countryside," was invited. "The whole house was thrown open to feasting: there were rices of five several colours, and sherbets of as many more; and kids stuffed with walnuts and almonds and pistachios and a camel-colt roasted whole. So they ate and drank and made mirth and merriment; and the bride was displayed in her seven dresses and one more, to the women, who could not take their eyes off her."

But then the bridegroom, Abu Hasan, "was summoned to the chamber where [his bride] sat enthroned; and he rose slowly and with dignity from his divan; but in so doing, for that he was over full of meat and drink, lo and behold! he let fly a fart, great and terrible. Thereupon each guest turned to his neighbour and talked aloud and made as though he had heard nothing, fearing for his life. But a consuming fire was lit in Abu Hasan's heart; so he pretended a call of nature; and, in lieu of seeking the bride-chamber, he went down to the housecourt and saddled his mare and rode off, weeping bitterly, through the shadow of the night."

Fleeing the country without even a goodbye, he heads for India to make a new life for himself. In those days there was always a king around, so in time Abu Hasan goes to work for a king, who "advanced him to the captainship of his bodyguard." In all, Abu Hasan lives ten prosperous years in India. But finally his nagging homesickness gets the better of him. As abruptly as he abandoned

---

Hillbillies Ned, Jerry, and Henry are bragging about how cold it is where they live. "It was so cold down in Washington Bottom this morning," Jerry says, "when I milked the cows I had to break off the streams of milk and stack 'em up like firewood."

"That's nothing," says Ned. "It was so cold up at Boaz, my wife tossed the dishwater out the back door and it froze in midair."

Henry spits a stream of tobacco juice. "Shit, that ain't nothin'. This morning it was so cold up at Worthington Creek that I farted on the way back to the house. Minute I got home I pulled down my pants and a green fuzzy ball of ice fell on the floor."

"What happened?" his buddies ask.

"Well, when I kicked it into the fireplace, it went pffffffffffttt!"

his own wedding banquet, now he departs from the king without a word and takes the long trip back home.

To avoid the shame he fears might still hang over his head, Abu Hasan dons the "rags" of a religious man as soon as his ship lands, and he walks to his old city "enduring a thousand hardships of hunger, thirst and fatigue; and braving a thousand dangers from the lion, the snake and the Ghul. But when he drew near his old home, he looked down upon it from the hills with brimming eyes, and said in himself, 'Haply they might know thee; so I will wander about the outskirts, and hearken to the folk. Allah grant that my case be not remembered by them!'"

After skulking around the suburbs incognito, he finds himself resting outside the door of a hut. He hears a young girl's voice inside asking, "O my mother, tell me the day when I was born." The mother replies, "Thou wast born, O my daughter, on the very night when Abu Hasan farted."

"Now the listener no sooner heard these words than he rose up from the bench, and fled away saying to himself, 'Verily thy fart hath become a date, which shall last for ever and ever. . . .' And he ceased not traveling and voyaging and returned to India; and there abode in self-exile till he died; and the mercy of Allah be upon him!"

Another tale within *The Arabian Nights* establishes the worth of a fart. It's called "Ja'Afar the Barmecide and the Old Badawi" (told by Scheherazade on the 395th night in Richard Burton's version), in which Ja'Afar encounters an elderly Bedouin (the Badawi) who is riding his donkey to Baghdad to seek a medical prescription for an eye ailment. Pulling the old traveler's leg, Ja'Afar offers him a remedy on the spot:

> Now lend me an ear and I will give thee a prescription, which
> I have given to none but thee. . . . Take three ounces of wind-
> breaths and the like of sunbeams and the same of moonshine
> and as much of lamp-light; mix them well together and let
> them lie in the wind three months. Then place them three
> months in a mortar without a bottom and pound them to
> fine powder and after trituration set them in a cleft platter,

and let it stand in the wind another three months; after which
use of this medicine three drachms every night in thy sleep,
and, Inshallah! thou shalt be healed and whole.

After patiently listening to this nonsense, the old man
"stretched himself out to full length on the donkey's back and let
fly a terrible loud fart and said to Ja'Afar, 'Take this fart in payment of thy prescription. When I have followed it, if Allah grant me
recovery, I will give thee a slave-girl . . . and when thou diest and
the Lord hurrieth thy soul to hell-fire, she shall blacken thy face
with her skite [shit].'"

Elsewhere in Burton's translation there are farts galore. In
"The Tale of Ali Nur el-Din and Miriam" (told on the 892nd night)
the king calls his youngest son "Fasyan [breaker of wind], sur-
named Salh al-Subyan [son of children's shit]." And in "Kamar al-
Zaman and the Jeweller's Wife" (on the 977th night), a pilgrim
sings of the privilege of being male, young and rich:

If generous youth be blessed with luck and wealth,
Displeasures fly his path and perils fleet:
His enviers pimp for him and par'site-wise
E'ven without tryst his mistress hastens to meet.
When loud he farts they say, "How well he sings!"
And when he fizzles cry they, "Oh, how sweet!"

Though the many poems, plays, stories, and passages in this
chapter are innocent and amusing, they were often censored over
the years by editors such as Thomas Bowdler (whose 1818 *Family
Shakespeare* was trimmed of "words and expressions . . . which are
so indecent in nature as to render it highly desirable that they should
be erased") or by translators who excluded the parts they or their
publishers disapproved of (often for practical reasons, considering
the fate of Zola's aforementioned publisher for not expurgating
enough) or who changed the meanings of words (Dr. Gilbert
Murray, translating Aristophanes' *Frogs* from classical Greek into
English in the nineteenth century, turned "breaking wind" into

"blowing one's nose"). And then of course there were the abbreviations f— or f—t. (In 1749, when Henry Fielding used "f—t" in his otherwise bawdy *The History of Tom Jones*, he sneaked in an actual fart anyway by adding: "Which last word he accompanied and graced with the very action.") To truly appreciate the pettiness of this censorship, simply try to read the bowdlerized version of Chaucer's "The Summoner's Tale"; without the old man farting in Friar John's hand and giving his "gift" to John's friary, the story is pointless.

This prudery carried on to include twentieth century writers. D. H. Lawrence's first major novel, *Sons and Lovers* (1913), was shorn of a fart passage by his editor, Edward Garnett; the fart—described in detail in a letter from the main character, Paul Morel, to his girlfriend Miriam Leivers—wasn't restored to the novel until a new edition was printed in 1992. Also, Helen T. Lowe-Porter's well-known translation of Thomas Mann's *Buddenbrooks* (1924) completely omitted all of Tony Buddenbrooks's son-in-law's farting scenes, which in essence gutted his character.

Nowadays, of course, very little if anything is censored, and all you have to do is crack open a book to find somebody farting. J. D. Salinger's *Catcher in the Rye*, Norman Mailer's *The Naked and the Dead*, and many modern classics include detailed farting scenes, many of them hilarious. In Joseph Wambaugh's *The Choirboys*, farting was a running joke that took on racial overtones ("It was a colored voice," one police lieutenant said after a cop farted in ranks; later, a black cop blasted "a terrible, vengeful fart" at a captain in the men's room and growled, "Take that, you jive turkey!"). Roald Dahl wrote a children's story called *The BFG*, in which the Big Friendly Giant, a likely descendant of Rabelais's Gargantua, breaks wind, which he calls "whizzpopping," at state occasions. In E. L. Doctorow's *Ragtime*, he wrote how Americans loved to overstuff themselves in the days of our only 300-pound president, William Howard Taft. "America was a farting country," Doctorow declared. John Irving's autobiographical *Hotel New Hampshire* (1981) includes a nice little piece of poetic justice: After an old dog is put to sleep because it farted too much and is then stuffed by a taxidermist, it falls out of a closet and frightens Irving's grandfather so badly that he suffers a fatal heart attack. The title of Don Zacharia's 1982 novel *The Match Trick* refers to lighting blue darters. Probably no modern novel stirred up a bigger shit storm than Gabriel Garcia Marquez's *The General in His Labyrinth* (1989), which portrays South America's "Great Liberator," Simon Bolivar, as, among other things, a guy with a serious farting problem.

A literary scholar could go on with this pedantic list of sulfuric sagas ad infartnitum, but you get the idea. Those who could cut the mustard as great writers could also cut the cheese.

FARTS SAVED THE WORLD FOR MANKIND

According to the March/April 1992 edition of *Science Frontiers*, paleontologists believe that farting dinosaurs significantly contributed to the earth's atmosphere and made the planet warmer. Throughout the 100-million-year Jurassic period, countless billions of lumbering dinosaurs like the mammoth brontosaurus spent nearly every waking hour of their lives munching on vegetation, which then wound its way in enormous amounts through their serpentine intestines for days or weeks, fermenting and digesting along the route, then literally escaping from their anuses as one continuous breeze, a silent fermata of farting that spewed nitrogren, hydrogren, carbon dioxide, methane, and other elemental gases into the air. In addition to making the climate friendlier for mammals, those eons of flatulence may have blown enough methane and hydrogren sulfide into the air to interrupt the dinosaurs' shell-forming glands and weaken their eggs.

6

A SWIFT KICK IN CUPID'S ASS

In doleful Scenes, that breaks our heart,
Punch comes, like you, and lets a Fart.

—Jonathan Swift,
Mad Mullinix and Timothy *(1728)*

This is a chapter that guys may find transcendent and women may despise. Just keep in mind that I'm simply the messenger, not the culprit, so don't shoot me.

The early eighteenth-century Anglo-Irish writer and poet Jonathan Swift, commonly known as Dr. Swift, is one of the English language's most renowned satirists. His most popular work, *Gulliver's Travels* (1726), is still beloved by millions, and his controversial essay *A Modest Proposal* (1729), a tongue-in-cheek suggestion of how Ireland could profitably reduce its glut of poor Catholic tots (written a full sixty years before Thomas Malthus's *Essay on Population*), continues to provoke, especially in a world that each day becomes more desperately overcrowded.

Along with the proper cooking of babies, Swift had a good deal to say about farting, generally as a weapon against pretension. In *An Excellent New Song* (1711) he wrote,

The duke shew'd me all his fine house; and the duchess
From her closet brought out a full purse in her clutches.

I talked of a peace, and they both gave a start,
His Grace swore by God, and Her Grace let a fart.

In 1729, when he and his friend Thomas Sheridan began publishing a weekly called the *Intelligencer*, Swift used his column to write scurrilous poetry about political enemies whom he turned into a cast of uncouth, gaseous characters, one of whom bragged in *Mad Mullinix and Timothy*, "I fart with twenty ladies by; they call me beast, and what care I?" In *Tom Mullinex and Dick*, Swift wrote, "Tom was held the merrier lad, but Dick the best at farting." Elsewhere, in *Dick's Variety*, "Dick can fart, and dance and frisk, no other monkey half so brisk."

One of Swift's targets was romantic love, that powerful mixture of worship and sexual fantasy that seems to possess so many young men. Between 1730 and 1734, Swift wrote several parodies of sentimental poetry that his contemporaries reviled even more than the misanthropy of *A Modest Proposal*. His biographer, Ricardo Quintana, called these verses "noxious compositions" driven by his "passion for . . . making the world see with eyes undimmed by folly and sentiment." Aldous Huxley, in 1929, even wrote an essay on them, damning Swift's "hatred of the bowels" and warning the reader to have "a bottle of smelling-salts handy, if you happen to be delicately stomached."

For example, in one of the poems, *Strephon and Chloe*, Swift wrote that it would have behooved the young lover Strephon, on the fateful day Chloe stole his heart, if he had "through a cranny spy'd on house of ease [his] future bride, in all the postures of her face . . . distortions, groanings, strainings, heavings"—in other words, if he could have peeked in and watched her taking a shit. Then all illusions of his madonna would be gone and Strephon could decide more objectively if Chloe was indeed a good companion for him. In Swift's words, it would be better to lick a woman's "leavings"—her shit—on the first date "than from experience find too late your goddess grown a filthy mate." An old Ladino (Judeo-Spanish) adage expresses the same sentiment: "If you come for the kisses, you must stay for the farts." The problem remains universal. At some point in every intimate relationship, somebody has to let the first turd splash and the first fart fly; only then can lovers settle into a mutual comfort zone.

Jonathan Swift humorously addressed the shattering of a young man's adoration in *Cassinus and Peter: A Tragical Elegy*, which begins as a mystery between two Cambridge students. Peter stops by Cassinus's dorm and finds him in bed, inconsolable and immobilized by depression, crying out the name of his beloved Celia. Asked if Celia has died, Cassinus says it's worse than that. "Come, tell us, has she play'd the whore?" No, it's worse even than that: "Nor can imagination guess," moans Cassinus, "nor eloquence divine express, how that ungrateful charming maid, my purest passion has betray'd. Conceive the most invenom'd dart, to pierce an injur'd lover's heart." Finally it all comes out how Cassinus discovered "Celia's foul disgrace," but he begs Peter to keep it a secret. "Nor wonder how I lost my wits; Oh! Celia, Celia, Celia shits."

Swift was no impudent adolescent when he wrote these romance parodies. He was a sexagenarian dean of St. Patrick's Cathedral in Dublin and a man of the world, albeit a cranky old fart, when he published *Cassinus and Peter* and *Strephon and Chloe*. But the age-old problem of romantic love, and the misogyny that often lies just beneath its surface, had been nibbling and gnawing at him for many years.

In his early thirties, in 1699, Swift wrote *The Problem*, an angry tale of cunning young women eager to accept a wealthy lord's fart as a facet of his passion—as if it were loaded with lust-provoking pheromones—and thus win his heart:

> Did ever problem thus perplex,
> Or more employ the female sex?
> So sweet a passion who cou'd think,
> Jove ever form'd to make a stink?
> The ladys vow, and swear they'll try,
> Whether it be a truth, or lye.
> Love's fire, it seems, like inward heat,
> Works in my Lord by stool and sweat,
> Which brings a stink from ev'ry pore,

And from behind, and from before;
Yet, what is wonderful to tell it,
None but the fav'rite nymph can smell it.
But now, to solve the nat'ral cause
By sober, philosophick laws,
Whether all passions, when in ferment,
Work out, as anger does in vermin?
So, when a weasel you torment,
You find his passion by his scent.
We read of kings, who in a fright,
Tho' on a throne, wou'd fall to shite.
Beside all this, deep scholars know,
That the main string of Cupid's bow,
Once on a time, was an asses gut,
Now to a nobler office put,
By favour, or desert preferr'd
From giving passage to a turd.
But still, tho' fixt among the stars,
Does sympathize with human arse.
Thus when you feel an hard-bound breech
Conclude love's bow-string at full stretch;
Till the kind looseness comes, and then
Conclude the bow relax'd again.
And now the ladys all are bent,
To try the great experiment;
Ambitious of a regent's heart
Spread all their charms to catch a fart;
Watching the first unsav'ry wind,
Some ply before, and some behind.
My Lord, on fire amidst the dames,
Farts like a laurel in the flames,
The fair approach the speaking part,
To try the back-way to his heart;
For, as when we a gun discharge,
Altho' the bore be ne'er so large,

Before the flame from muzzle burst,
Just at the breech it flashes first:
So from my Lord his passion broke,
He farted first, and then he spoke.
The Ladys vanish, in the smother,
To confer notes with one another;
And now they all agree, to name
Whom each one thought the happy dame:
Quoth Neal, whate'er the rest may think,
I'm sure, 'twas I that smelt the stink.
You smell the stink? by God you lye,
Quoth Ross, for, I'll be sworn, 'twas I.
Ladys, quoth Levens, pray forbear,
Let's not fall out; we all had share.
And, by the most we can discover,
My Lord's an universal lover.

Swift introduced Celia, the woman whose act of shitting so discombobulated Cassinus, to the callow Strephon (apparently before he met Chloe) in *The Lady's Dressing Room* (1730). Like Cassinus, Strephon had a hard time dealing with the unglamorous truth he found behind the facade of femininity when he investigated Celia's inner sanctum:

Five hours, (and who can do it less in?)
By haughty *Celia* spent in dressing;
The goddess from her chamber issues,
Array'd in lace, brocade and tissues.
Strephon, who found the room was void,
And *Betty* [Celia's maid] otherwise employ'd;
Stole in, and took a strict survey,
Of all the litter as it lay;
Whereof, to make the matter clear,
An inventory follows here.

Strephon goes through Celia's things, noting the sweat stains in the armpits of her dirty smock, the dirt in her combs, the "allum flower to stop the steams, exhal'd from sour unsavory streams," the ointments for scabs, a hand basin filled with filthy water, mildewed towels gummed with grime and earwax, snotty handkerchiefs, stinking stockings, tweezers and greasy hairpins. But the worst comes when he opens the "Pandora's box" of Celia's toilet chest:

So *Strephon* lifting up the lid,
To view what in the chest was hid,
The vapours flew from out the vent,
But *Strephon* cautious never meant
The bottom of the pan to grope,
And fowl his hands in search of hope.
O ne'er may such a vile machine
Be once in *Celia*'s chamber seen!
O may she better learn to keep
"Those secrets of the hoary deep!"
. . . .
And up exhales a greasy stench,
For which you curse the careless wench;
So things, which must not be exprest,
When plumpt into the reeking chest;
Send up an excremental smell
To taint the parts from whence they fell.
The pettycoats and gown perfume,
And waft a stink round every room.
But Vengeance, goddess never sleeping
Soon punish'd *Strephon* for his peeping;
His foul imagination links
Each dame he sees with all her stinks:
And, if unsav'ry odours fly,
Conceives a lady standing by
. . . .
I pity wretched *Strephon* blind
To all the charms of womankind;

Should I the queen of love refuse,
Because she rose from stinking ooze?

But in the end, Swift hopes that Strephon will grow up and accept the earthly woman behind the fanciful imago:

When *Celia* in her glory shows,
If *Strephon* would but stop his nose

He soon would learn to think like me,
And bless his ravisht eyes to see
Such order from confusion sprung,
Such gaudy tulips rais'd from dung.

Which brings us to when Strephon met Chloe (*Strephon and Chloe*) in 1734. Jonathan Swift delivered his best poesy on the subject of infatuation thrown into the dirt—then salvaged as love:

Of *Chloe* all the town has rung;
By ev'ry size of poets sung:
So beautiful a nymph appears
But once in twenty thousand years.
By nature form'd with nicest care,
And, faultless to a single hair.
Her graceful mein, her shape, and face,
Confest her of no mortal race:
And then, so nice, and so genteel;
Such cleanliness from head to heel:
No humours gross, or frowsy steams,
No noisome whiffs, or sweaty streams,
Before, behind, above, below,
Could from her taintless body flow.
Would so discreetly things dispose,
None ever saw her pluck a rose.
Her dearest comrades never caught her

Squat on her hams, to make maid's water.
You'd swear, that so divine a creature
Felt no necessities of nature.

Thus we meet Chloe, the bride. But the groom, Strephon, is a young man so ashamed of his own earthliness in the presence of this beautiful woman that he worries "How with so high a nymph he might demean himself the wedding-night: For, as he view'd his person round, meer mortal flesh was all he found."

But Swift reminds us that once a man and his goddess are confined to the same room with all social separation stripped away, more than feet turn into clay.

Now, ponder well ye parents dear;
Forbid your daughters guzzling beer;
And make them ev'ry afternoon
Forbear their tea, or drink it soon;
That, e'er to bed they venture up,
They may discharge it ev'ry sup;
If not; they must in evil plight
Be often forc'd to rise at night,
Keep them to wholsome food confin'd,
Nor let them taste what causes wind;
('Tis this the sage of *Samos** means,
Forbidding his disciples beans)
. . . .
But, out it flies, even when she meets
Her bridegroom in the wedding-sheets.
Carminative and *diuretick*
Will damp all passion sympathetick;
And, love such nicety requires,
One *blast* will put out all his fires.

* The Greek philosopher Pythagoras. See Chapter 2.

71

As it turns out, Chloe's parents hadn't warned her against eating legumes and drinking tea before the wedding party, so things turn sour as soon as she and Strephon climb into their honeymoon bed.

Twelve cups of tea, (with grief I speak)
Had now constrain'd the nymph to leak.
This point must needs be settled first;
The bride must either void or burst.
Then, see the dire effect of pease,
Think what can give the colick ease,
The nymph opprest before, behind,
As ships are toss't by waves and wind,
Steals out her hand by nature led,
And brings a vessel into bed:
Fair utensil, as smooth and white
As *Chloe*'s skin, almost as bright.
Strephon who heard the fuming rill
As from a mossy cliff distill;
Cry'd out, ye gods, what sound is this?
Can *Chloe*, heav'ly *Chloe* piss?
But, when he smelt a noysom steam
Which oft attends that luke-warm stream

. . . .

And, though contriv'd, we may suppose
To slip his ears, yet struck his nose:
He found her, while the scent increas'd,
As *mortal* as himself, at least.
But, soon with like occasions prest,
He boldly sent his hand in quest,
(Inspir'd with courage from his bride,)
To reach the pot on t'other side.
And as he fill'd the reeking vase,
Let fly a rouzer in her face.
The little *Cupids* hov'ring round,

(As pictures prove) with garlands crown'd,
Abasht at what they saw and heard,
Flew off, nor evermore appear'd.

But all is well between Strephon and Chloe, because they no longer have to worry about pissing, shitting, and farting in each other's presence; each can delight in the other's bodily functions:

How great a change! how quickly made!
They learn to call a spade, a spade.
They soon from all constraint are freed;
Can see each other *do their need*.
On box of cedar sits the wife,
And makes it warm for *dearest life*.
And, by the beastly way of thinking,
Find great society in stinking.
Now *Strephon* daily entertains
His *Chloe* in the homeli'st strains;
And, Chloe, more experienc'd grown,
With int'rest pays him back his own.
No maid at court is less asham'd,
Howe'er for selling bargains fam'd,
Than she, to name her parts behind,
or when a-bed, to let out wind.

And so we leave them, farting at each other as heartily as college boys in a cutting contest. Ah, that Jonathan Swift sure knew a thing or two about love.

FARTS MAY BE THE DEATH OF MANKIND

Thanks to the output of gazillions of cellulose-munching microbes that live in cow stomachs, the collective farting of the world's 1.3 billion cattle annually expels "nearly 100 million metric tons of methane—a powerful greenhouse gas," into the atmosphere, according to the editors of a book called *50 Simple Things You Can Do to Save the Earth*. Earth Save, a California organization that wants a "major reduction" in the world's cattle population, puts the number even higher, at 500 million metric tons. Other sources compute lower figures, from 85 million tons down to 38.6 million, but that's still nothing to sniff at. Scientists, including Dr. S. Fred Singer, who first alerted the world to the danger of cow farts in 1971, say that the growing abundance of methane in our atmosphere could someday make the earth inhospitable for human civilization. In 1990 the Environmental Protection Agency reported that after rice paddies, ruminant animals are the world's largest producers of methane, accounting for 12 to 15 percent of emissions. (Naturally the National Cattlemen's Association rushed forward with its own numbers, claiming that cow farts and cow pies were responsible for less than 0.5 percent of new methane being released into the atmosphere.) Iowa state senator Charles E. Grassley proposed that since cows are so flatulent, they should be fitted with airbags, complete with catalytic converters, to harness this huge source of energy. "And if that does not work in reducing cow methane gas emissions, we can tax them," Grassley said. "Call it another gas tax."

(Elephants actually fart more than twice as much as cows do. The average pachyderm poots over a million cubic centimeters of methane each day—enough to keep an automobile moving for twenty miles—compared to a mere 300,000 to 600,000 cubic centimeters for the average backfiring bovine, but there are far fewer elephants in the world than cows. The average human contributes a mere 400 to 1,200 cc's of gas each day.)

But wait! According to the November 5, 1982, issue of Science, the National Center for Atmospheric Research in Boulder, Colorado, reported that tiny termites are the biggest polluters of all, microfarting not only 150 million tons of methane annually into the air as they chew their way through wooden buildings, forests, and other vegetable matter, but also more carbon dioxide than is produced by all the world's smokestacks. Seem farfetched? Keep in mind that for every human being on this planet, there are three quarters of a ton of termites, according to scientist James P. Greenberg, and that's a lot of tiny assholes.

But lest we blame the world's toxic fart fumes on cows and termites, we should remember foremost that the human race has designed complex farting surrogates, such as internal-combustion engines and smokestack industries ("Amalgamated Fart," comedian Robert Klein once called them), that dump our own noxious gases into the atmosphere. Think of your car's exhaust pipe as a mere extension of your own farting anus.

7

MEN OF LETTERS: MARK TWAIN
AND BEN FRANKLIN SPELL F-A-R-T!

At Thunder now no more I start,
Than at the whisp'ring of a Fart.

—*Poor Richard, "On His Deafness" (c. 1750)*

In the right hands, the fart is mightier than the sword. (It's also sharper, because it cuts through the seat of your pants without making a hole.) At a moment in each of their lives, two American heroes—statesman-inventor Benjamin Franklin and author Mark Twain—felt that flatulence was the only way to get a point across. Both of them wrote personal letters that satirized the stuffiness of the academic and scientific communities. One was a one-act play, the other a treatise. One was subsequently published by the author himself, the other languished for 150 years before seeing the light of day.

Our journey begins about seventy years ago, when someone accidentally discovered in the Library of Congress, in Washington, D.C., a dusty old letter that Ben Franklin had written from Paris in 1783, to a friend in America named Dr. Richard Pierce. Tucked within the correspondence was a longer paper that Franklin had written two years earlier, when he was a seventy-five-year-old eminence whose experiments, theories, and opinions were familiar in scientific circles throughout America and Europe.

"Inflammable Air puts me in mind of a little jocular paper I wrote some years since in ridicule of a prize Question given out on this side of the Water," Franklin told Dr. Pierce, "and I enclose it for your Amusement."

Originally untitled, Franklin's paper became known as *The Letter to a Royal Academy* when it was published in an underground pamphlet in the 1920s, and it has been snickered over ever since.

Franklin's inspiration was an annual prize question contest sponsored by the Royal Academy of Brussels, an international scientific organization. In years past, the academy had posed hypothetical problems concerning "natural philosophy." But suddenly the board of scientists abandoned the theoretical realm because it lacked "utility" and had no value to the real world. According to the new policy, the prize question had to be a practical, empirical conundrum.

In response, Ben Franklin wrote a facetious proposal to the "learned Physicians, Chemists, etc." of the Royal Academy, suggesting a question that was philosophical but at the same time useful to everyday life: Could science find a way to make farts more piquant?—you know, smell better.

Let Mr. Franklin speak for himself:

It is universally well known, That in digesting our common Food, there is created or produced in the Bowels of human Creatures, a great Quantity of Wind.

That the permitting this Air to escape and mix with the Atmosphere, is usually offensive to the Company, from the fetid Smell that accompanies it.

That all well-bred People therefore, to avoid giving such Offence, forcibly restrain the Efforts of Nature to discharge that Wind.

That so retained contrary to Nature, it not only gives frequently great present Pain, but occasions future Diseases, such as habitual Cholics, Ruptures, Tympanies, &c., often destructive of the Constitution, & sometimes of Life itself.

Were it not for the odiously offensive Smell accompanying such Escapes, polite People would probably be under no more Restraint in discharging such Wind in Company, than they are in spitting, or in blowing their Noses.

My Prize Question therefore should be, *To discover some Drug wholesome and not disagreeable, to be mixed with our common Food, or Sauces, that shall render the Natural Discharges, of Wind from our Bodies, not only inoffensive, but agreeable as Perfumes.*

That this is not a chimerical Project, and altogether impossible, may appear from these Considerations. That we already have some Knowledge of Means capable of Varying that Smell. He that dines on stale Flesh, especially with much Addition of Onions, shall be able to afford a Stink that no Company can tolerate; while he that has lived for some Time on Vegetables only, shall have that Breath so pure as to be insensible to the most delicate Noses; and if he can manage so as to avoid the Report, he may any where give Vent to his Griefs, unnoticed. But as there are many to whom an entire Vegetable Diet would be inconvenient, and as a little Quick-Lime thrown into a Jakes [outhouse] will correct the amazing Quantity of fetid Air arising from the vast Mass of putrid Matter contained in such Places, and render it rather pleasing to the Smell, who knows but that a little Powder of Lime (or some other thing equivalent) taken in our Food, or perhaps a Glass of Limewater drank at Dinner, may have the same Effect on the Air produced in and issuing from our Bowels? This is worth the Experiment.

Certain it is also that we have the Power of changing by slight Means the Smell of another Discharge, that of our Water. A few Stems of Asparagus eaten, shall give our Urine a disagreeable Odour; and a Pill of Turpentine no bigger than a Pea, shall bestow on it the pleasing Smell of Violets. And why should it be thought more impossible in Nature, to find Means of making a Perfume of our *Wind* than of our *Water?*

For the Encouragement of this Enquiry (from the immortal Honour to be reasonably expected by the Inventor), let it be reasonably considered of how small Importance of Mankind,

or to how small a Part of Mankind have been useful those
Discoveries in Science that have heretofore made
Philosophers famous. Are there twenty Men in Europe at this
Day, the happier, or even the easier, for any Knowledge they
have picked out of Aristotle? What Comfort can the Vortices
of Descartes give to a Man who has Whirlwinds in his
Bowels! The Knowledge of Newton's Mutual *Attraction* of
the Particles of Matter, can it afford Ease to him who is
racked by their mutual *Repulsion*, and the cruel Distensions
it occasions? The Pleasure arising to a few Philosophers, from
seeing, a few Times in their Life, the Threads of Light
untwisted, and separated by the Newtonian Prism into seven
Colours, can it be compared with the Ease and Comfort
every Man living might feel seven times a Day, by discharging
freely the Wind from his Bowels? Especially if it be converted
into a Perfume: For the Pleasure of one Sense being little infe-
rior to those of another, instead of pleasing the *Sight* he
might delight the *Smell* of those about him, & make
Numbers happy, which to a benevolent Mind must afford
infinite Satisfaction. The generous Soul, who now endeavours
to find out whether the Friends he entertains like best Claret
or Burgundy, Champagne or Madeira, would then enquire
also whether they chose Musk or Lilly, Rose or Bergamot,
and provide accordingly. And surely such a Liberty of *Ex-
pressing* one's *Scenti-ments*, and *pleasing one another*, is of
infinitely more Importance to human Happiness than that
Liberty of the *Press*, or *of abusing one another*, which the
English are so ready to fight & die for.

In short, this Invention, if compleated, would be, as Bacon
expresses it, *bringing Philosophy home to Men's Business and
Bosoms.* And I cannot but conclude, that in Comparison
therewith, for *universal* and *continual* Utility, the Science of
the Philosophers abovementioned, even with the Addition,
Gentlemen, of your '*Figure quelconque*' and the Figures
inscribed in it, are, all together, scarcely worth a FART*hing.*"

As he wrote this treatise, Ben Franklin might have been thinking of *Means of Succeeding*, a French best-seller in 1610 by
Francois Beroalde de Verville, who described the exploits of a
sixteenth-century courtesan in a chapter called "A Tale of Fair
Imperia." "The Lord of Lierne, a French gentleman, went to bed
with a courtesan in Rome," de Verville wrote.

> As chaste courtesans well know their business, she had pro-
> cured some little pellicules which had been filled with scented
> air through the skill of perfumers. Having a supply of these
> wares and holding the gentleman in her arms, the good
> Imperia allowed herself to be loved. To add an edge to the
> fondling and to draw her lover more closely, the lady took
> one of the pellicules in her hand and burst it, thus making the
> audible sound of a fart. On hearing this the gentleman with-
> drew his head from the bed to give himself air. "It's not what
> you think," she said, "You must [smell] before being afraid."
> Thus persuaded he received an agreeable odor quite contrary
> to what he had expected and which he savoured with plea-
> sure. This having been repeated a number of times, he
> enquired of the lady if such winds proceeded from her con-
> sidering that they smelt so good and given the fact that simi-
> lar winds emanating from the lower portions of French ladies
> were stinking and abominable. To this she replied with a little
> frisky philosophy to the effect that Italian ladies, due to the
> nature of the country and the aromatic food and to the use of
> odoriferous articles, produced their quintessence in the lower
> regions as if it were the neck of a retort. "In truth," he
> replied, "our own ladies fart in a quite different way."
> It so happened that after some more musketry and on
> account of withholding her wind for so long, Imperia farted
> naturally, substantially and at length. The Frenchman dili-
> gently stuck his nose under the sheets in order to apprehend
> the good odour which he wished to savor to the full. But he
> was deceived; he received through his nose a stench of barn-

yard proportions. "Oh! my dear lady," he said, "what have you done?" She answered, "My lord, I was but paying you a compliment to remind you of your own country."

(The idea of scented farts was carried on in a Jim Carrey skit in a 1990 episode of the Fox TV show *In Living Color*. See chapter 10.)

From 1733 through 1758, Ben Franklin also wrote and published under the pseudonym Richard Saunders a successful magazine called *Poor Richard's Almanack*. As Poor Richard, Franklin dispensed practical advice and pearls of wisdom, the most familiar being "Early to Bed, and early to rise, makes a Man healthy, wealthy and wise." But he was not above scenting his aphorisms with flatulence. For example, in 1751 he wrote, "He that is conscious of a Stink in his Breeches is jealous of every Wrinkle in another's Nose." As an adjunct to the adage "Industry need not wish," Richard wrote, "He that lives upon Hope will die farting."

Meanwhile, science has not yet solved the problem of smelly fart gas. The search for what poet e.e. cummings in 1940 called "the splendor of an angel's fart" goes on.

Humorist Samuel L. Clemens, better known as Mark Twain, was concerned more with protesting against Victorian censorship

AMERICA'S FOREFATHERS BLEW A FEATHER OUT THEIR ASS AND CALLED IT MACARONI

"Yankee Doodle," a popular song from the 1760s, was originally a derisive anti-American ditty that the British Army played to irritate New England colonists. *Doodle* referred to either a penis or a numbskull. But after provincial sharpshooters humiliated retreating Redcoats along the forested Lexington-Arlington Road by killing or wounding well over 200 soldiers without suffering a casualty, the American revolutionaries expropriated "Yankee Doodle" as their own "to emphasize the magnitude of the British defeat" and turned a song of derision into an anthem of defiance, according to historian Kenneth Silverman. Before the familiar patriotic lyrics were added to the music around 1776, some of the original words to "Yankee Doodle" were: "Dolly Bushel let a Fart, Jenny Jones she found it, Ambrose carried it to the Mill, Where Doctor Warren ground it."

than with tweaking the noses of stuffy scientists. Inspired by a real fart that Edward de Vere, the seventeenth earl of Oxford, reportedly let slip while bowing to Queen Elizabeth nearly 300 years earlier, Twain wrote a one-act play called *1601*—now known more commonly as *A Fart in Queen Elizabeth's Court*. Twain may also have been thinking about a fart that Henry Ludlow blasted as a no vote in Parliament in 1607. That celebrated crepitation had already been enshrined by several poems, including Ben Jonson's "Epigram 133: On the Famous Voyage" (1616) and Sir John Mennis's "The Fart Censured in the Parliament House" (1656).

Or Twain may have been thinking about a lesser-known personage named Jack of Dover, who wrote in a chapter called "The Fool of Cornwall" in a 1604 pamphlet called *Quest of Inquiry*,

> I was told of a humorous knight dwelling in . . . Cornwall,
> who upon a time, having gathered together in one open
> market-place a great assemblie of knights, squires, gentlemen,
> and yeomen, and whilest they stood expecting to heare some
> discourse or speech to proceed from him, he, in a foolish man-
> ner not without laughter, began to use a thousand jestures,
> turning his eyes this way and then that way, seeming always
> as though presently he would have begun to speake, and at
> last, fetching a deepe sigh, with a grunt like a hogge, he let a
> beastly loud fart, and tould them that the occasion of this call-
> ing them together was to no other end but that so noble a fart
> might be honored with so noble a company as there was.

In any event, Mark Twain's crepitation classic began as a private letter he wrote to his best friend, Reverend Joseph Twichell, in 1876, while Twain was researching his next book, *The Prince and the Pauper*. In an attempt to practice his "archaics" he contrived a conversation within Queen Elizabeth's court. After polishing the script over the next couple of years, Twain privately published four copies in 1880 under the title *1601*. In 1882 the first authorized edition—fifty copies in book form—was printed by the U.S. Military Academy Press at West Point, with an added subtitle: *Conversation, as It Was by the Social Fireside in the Time of the Tudors*. Various underground publishers have kept it in print ever since.

In the mid-1890s, during an autobiographical musing, Twain gave some insight into the fictional narrator of *1601*: "The Queen's cup-bearer, a dried-up old nobleman, was present to take down the talk—not that he wanted to do it but because it was the Queen's desire and he had to. He loathed all those people because they were of offensively low birth, and because they hadn't a thing to recommend them except their incomparable brains. . . . I put into the Queen's mouth, and into the mouths of those other people, grossness not to be found outside of Rabelais, perhaps."

Written in exaggerated Elizabethan English, complete with arbitrary spellings (which I've left intact here) and capitalized nouns, *1601* takes us into a gathering of notables, including Ben Jonson, Will Shakespeare (Shaxpur), Sir Francis Bacon, and Sir Walter Raleigh, in the presence of Queen Elizabeth and her court. Rather than describe the play or highlight its most foul-smelling parts, I present its first half for your approval and amusement, as Mark Twain himself published it (with some translations added in brackets) over a century ago:

> Yesternight toke her maiste ye queene [*majesty the queen*] a
> fantasie such as she sometimes hath, and hadde to her closet
> certain that doe write playes, bokes, and such like, these
> being my lord Bacon, his worship Sr Walter Ralegh, Mr. Ben
> Jonson, and ye childe Francis Beaumonte, which being but
> sixteen, hath yet turned his hande to ye doing of ye Lattin
> masters into our Englishe tonge, wh [*with*] grete discretion
> and much applaus. Also came wh these ye famous Shaxpur. A
> righte straunge mixing truly of mightie blode wh mean, ye
> more in especial since ye queenes grace was present, as like-
> wise these following, to wit: Ye Duchess of Bilgewater, twenty-
> two yeres of age; ye Countesse of Granby, twenty-six; her
> doter, ye Lady Helen, fifteen; as also these two maides of
> honour, to wit: ye Lady Margery Boothy, sixty-five, and ye
> Lady Alice Dilberry, turned seventy, she being two yeres ye
> queenes graces elder.

I being her maistes cup-bearer, hadde no choice but to remaine and beholde rank forgot, and ye high holde converse wh ye low as uppon equal termes, a grete scandal did ye world heare therof.

In ye heat of ye talk it befel yt [*that*] one did breake wynde, yielding an exceding mightie and distresful stink, wherat all did laffe full sore, and then—

Ye Queene.—Verily in mine eight and sixty yeres have I not heard the fellow to this fart. Meseemeth, by ye grete sounde and clamour of it, it was male; yet ye belly it did lurk behinde shoulde now fall leane and flat against ye spine of him yt hath bene delivered of so stately and so vaste a bulk, wheras ye guts of them yt doe quiff-splitters [*penises*] beare, stande comely still and rounde. Prithee let ye author confes ye offspring. Will my Lady Alice testify?

Lady Alice.—Good your grace, an' [*if*] I hadde room for such a thunderbust within mine ancient bowels, 'tis not in reason I coulde discharge ye same and live to thank God for yt He did chose handmaide so humble wherby to shew his power. Nay, 'tis not I yt have broughte forth this rich o'ermastering fog, this fragrant bloom, so pray ye seeke ye further.

Ye Queene.—Mayhap ye Lady Margery hath done ye companie this favour?

Lady Margery.—So please ye madam, my limbs are feeble wh ye weighte and drouth of five and sixty winters, and it behoveth yt I be tender unto them. In ye good providence of God, an' *I* hadde contained this wonder, forsoothe wolde I have gi'en ye whole evening of my sinking life to ye dribbling of it forth, wh trembling and uneasy soul, not launched it sudden in its matchless might, taking mine own life wh violence, rending my weak frame like rotten rags. It was not I, your maiste.

Ye Queene.—O' God's name who hath favoured us? Hath it come to pass yt a fart shall fart *itself*? Not such a one as this, I trow. Young Master Beaumonte—but no; 'twolde have

wafted him to heav'n like downe of gooses boddy. 'Twas not
ye little Lady Helen-nay, ne'er blush, my childe; thoul't tickle
thy tender maidenhedde with many a mousie-squeak before
thou learnest to blow a harricane like this. Was't you, my
learned and ingenious Jonson?

Jonson.—So fell a blast hath ne'er mine ears salute, nor yet
a stench so all-pervading and immortal. 'Twas not a novice
did it, good your maiste, but one of veteran experience—else
hadde he failed of confidence. In sooth it was not I.

Ye Queene.—My lord Bacon?

Lord Bacon.—Not from mine leane entrailes hath this
prodigie burst forth, so pleas your grace. Naught doth so
befit ye grete as grete performance; and haply shall ye find yt
'tis not from mediocrity this miracle hath issued.

(Tho' ye subject be but a fart, yet will this tedious sink of
learning pondrously phillosophize. Meantime did the foul
and deadly stink pervade all places to that degree, yt never
smelt I ye like, yet dare I not to leave ye presence, albeit I was
like to suffocate.)

Ye Queene.—What saith ye worshipful Master Shaxpur?

Shaxpur.—In the grete hand of God I stande and so proclaim mine innocence. Though ye sinless hosts of heav'n
hadde foretolde ye coming of this most desolating breath,
proclaiming it a work of uninspired man, its quaking thunders, its firmament-clogging rottenness, its own achievement
in due course of nature, yet hadde not I believed it; but hadde
said the pit itself hath furnished forth the stink, and heav'ns
artillery hath shook the globe in admiration of it.

(Then there was a silence, and each did turn him toward the
worshipful Sr Walter Ralegh that browned, embattled, bloody
swashbuckler, who rising up did smile, and simpering say)

Sr W.—Most gracious maiste, 'twas I that did it, but indeed
it was so poor and frail a note, compared wh such as I am
wont to furnish, yt in sooth I was ashamed to call the weakling
mine in so august a presence. It was nothing—less than noth-

ing, madam—I did it but to clear my nether throat; but hadde I come prepared, then hadde I delivered something worthie. Bear wh me, pleas your grace, till I can make amends.

(Then delivered he himself of such a godless and rock-shivering blast that all were fain to stoppe their ears, and following it did come so dense and foul a stink that yt which went before did seem a poor and trifling thing beside it. Then saith he, feigning that he blushed and was confused, *I perceive that I am weak to-day, and cannot justice do unto my powers*: and sat him down as who shoulde say, *There it is not much; yet he yt hath an arse to spare, let him fellow yt, an think he can.* By God, an I were ye Queene, I wolde e'ev tip this swaggering braggart out o' the court, and let him air his grandeurs and break his intolerable wynde before ye deaf and such as suffocation pleaseth.)

From there the conversation in *1601* turned to explicit sexual matters, until "ye blodie bucanier hadde got his secconde wynde, and did turn his mind to farting wh such villain zeal that presently I was like to choke once more. God damn this wyndie ruffian and all his breed. I wolde yt hell mighte get him."

As for Edward de Vere, the real-life courtier in Queen Elizabeth's court, he was so ashamed and abashed by his gastric *faux pas* (much like the character Abu Hasan in *The Arabian Nights*) that he left England and traveled abroad for seven years. However, "on his returne," wrote Vere's seventeenth-century biographer James Aubrey, "the Queen welcomed him home, and say'd, 'My Lord, I had forgot the Fart.'"

And returning to Lord Henry Ludlow's cracking nay vote in the house of Parliament in 1607, Ben Jonson felt that "it was th'intent of the grave fart, late let in parliament, had it beene seconded, and not in fume vanish'd away." According to the poet Sir John Mennis, "it gave a foule knock, as it launch'd forth from [Ludlow's] stinking dock," and was sent "as a traitor, to the Tower [of London] . . . where as they say, it remaines to this houre, yet not close prisoner, but at large in the Tower."

YOU CAN FART BUT YOU CAN'T HIDE

Many jokes are about people who only think they're getting away with sneaking out a fart. For example, a young pianist is trying to impress the beautiful daughter of a prominent family by playing his own compositions on her piano. Suddenly feeling an uncontrollable urge to fart, he tells the lovely girl that he's written a new song just for her called "The Storm." His fingers begin to ripple across the keys, and each time he has to squeeze off a one-cheek sneak, he hammers loudly on the bass keys to imitate thunder. Afterward, he asks her if she'd like to hear it again.

"Yes," she murmurs sweetly, "but this time could you please leave out the part where the lightning hits the shithouse!"

In a variation on that joke, a young man is visiting his girlfriend's parents for the first time. Understandably nervous as he sits with them at the dinner table, he needs to let out some gas. Luckily for him, the family dog, Buck, comes over begging to be petted, so he slips out a fart and waves a hand in the air a couple of times as he tells the overly friendly dog, "Go on, Buck, that's enough." After this happens a couple more times, the father adds, "Do what he says, Buck, before he shits on you."

In perhaps a funnier version, a door-to-door cosmetics saleswoman gets on the elevator after making her rounds on the top floor of a high rise apartment building. She pushes the button for the ground floor, and the moment the doors shut she lets loose with an industrial-strength fart she's been holding in for the past half hour. Opening her display case, she grabs a sample can of pine-scent air freshener and sprays all around the elevator. Suddenly it stops on the sixth floor and a guy gets on. He visibly takes a couple of whiffs.

To see how well her product is working, the saleslady asks, "Is that a new kind of pine scent in here?"

"Either that," he replies, "or you just shit a Christmas tree."

Finally, in a nice twist on this theme, Queen Elizabeth and the archbishop of Canterbury are touring the royal stables, admiring the horses, when Her Majesty involuntarily lets a fart slip out. Unsure of whether the clergyman heard her delicate breakage or not, she lightly apologizes by saying, "Oh, I'm sorry."

The archbishop, waving his hands frantically in front of his nose, says, "Your Majesty needn't apologize for one of the royal steeds."

8

Religious Farts

Get thee behind me, Satan.

—*Jesus Christ, Mark 8:33, Matthew 16:23*
and Luke 4:8

When I was a kid, the pastor at our church exhorted us to "make a joyful noise unto the Lord." Well, what noise is more joyous than a robust fart, especially after you've been sitting on a hard pew for an hour digesting a breakfast of eggs, biscuits, and gravy?

But farting in church was always one of the big no-nos. This proscription goes way back before Christianity really got started. Around A.D. 98, Martial, the Roman epigrammatist, wrote:

As Aethon was praying to Jove
in the temple one day,
his eyes turned to heaven
and standing on the tips of his toes,
unlucky Aethon happened to fart.
The men around him laughed,
but the head of the gods became affronted,
and punished the blushing sinner
by making him fast for three days.

Ever since this outrage
miserable Aethon,
whenever he wants to enter
the Temple of Jove
first goes to the toilets nearby
and there he farts
maybe ten or twenty times.
And yet,
in spite of all these windy precautions
Aethon still addresses Jove
always holding tightly closed
his asshole.
(*Epigrams* 12, 77)

As it turns out, the human asshole has held grave importance
in most religions. It is the source of the foul-smelling shit and gas
that constantly admonish us for our perditious sin and lowly
humanity. Since we cannot see our assholes, they are exposed to
sinister forces that may possess us from behind and below. If this
explanation seems far-fetched, look no further than Martin Luther,
the early German nationalist and theologian who lit the fires of the
Reformation and Protestant Christianity when he nailed his ninety-
five Theses, mostly complaints against the Catholic Church, to the
door of Frederick's Castle Church at Wittenberg in 1517.

Martin Luther claimed to have been first visited by the Holy
Spirit while he was taking a shit. During his many table talks, as his
rambling speeches were being transcribed by monks, he waxed scatological as he scolded sinners, railed against his adversaries (he
referred to Governor Ferneze of Malta as *Furzesel*—the German
word for "fart-ass") and recounted his encounters with Satan.
"The only portion of the human anatomy which the pope has had
to leave uncontrolled is the hind end," Luther said, implying that
the Devil had seized this nether region for his own. ("May the devil
take the hindmost," is a common expression.) According to Luther,
the Devil expressed his scorn for mankind by baring his bunghole
and shitting or farting. "A Christian should and could be happy,"

he said, "but then the Devil shits on him." Luther also made wood-cut sketches of small demons being forcefully expelled from the Devil's asshole like fart-blasted dingleberries.

These ideas didn't originate with Martin Luther. Two hundred years earlier, in an anonymous, farcical fourteenth-century fable called *Le Muynier*, John Bourke told of a miller who believed in a peculiar philosophy then current that, at the moment of death, when the bowels go slack, a man's soul escaped by way of his ass-hole. When the miller lay upon his deathbed, he warned his wife and his priest to go away because he was "about to besmirch" him-self. Ignoring his protests, they pulled him to the edge of the bed and turned him on his side so that they could witness his final fart. Just as the gas began to erupt from between the poor miller's butt cheeks, a demon materialized, caught the fart in a sack and flew off in a sulfurous vapor before the priest could stop him.

Turnabout was fair play: According to Martin Luther, any mortal man could beat the Devil at his own game by baring his ass and telling Ol' Scratch to kiss it, or—better yet—farting into the Devil's nostrils. Satan can't stand rotten odors, he said, even though the Devil's own brimstone (sulfur) is a component of flatulence. "But if that is not enough for you, you Devil," Luther added at one point, "I have also shit and pissed; wipe your mouth on that and take a hearty bite." Luther also bragged that he had once given Satan "a fart for a staff" to lean on.

Satan's own flatulence was a familiar motif in medieval Christianity and storytelling. In Chaucer's prologue to "The Summoner's Tale," the summoner insults his fellow pilgrim, a friar, with a joke in which Satan holds up his pointed tail to show where friars come from. "And in less than a minute," wrote Chaucer, "just as bees swarm from a hive, so twenty thousand friars rushed in a line from the devil's ass and swarmed all over hell." Ben Jonson's "Ballad of Cock Lorel"—included in chapter 5—had the devil eating members of London's mercantile society and farting them out in one huge butt-blast. And in dramatist Phillip Massinger's 1632 play *The Maid of Honor*, a knight of Malta named Gonzaga declares, "I'll mumble a prayer or two, and cross myself, and then, tho' the Devil fart fire, have at him!"

In fact, the word *pumpernickel* comes from "devil's fart" in German. *Pumpern* means "to fart" and *nickel* is a "devil" or "goblin." The idea, according to etymologist Martha Barnette, was that dark, heavy pumpernickel bread could "produce outbursts of flatulence as powerful as those of the Devil himself."

But farts could also fool Satan. In his 1965 autobiography, surrealist painter Salvador Dali included a translation of an excerpt from a nineteenth-century manuscript called *The Art of Farting*, or *The Sly Artilleryman's Manual*, by Count Trumpet, about a modern-day bedeviled Faust. No longer able to resist the Devil pestering him for his soul, this poor man finally capitulated, but "on three conditions which he put to [Satan] there and then." First the man asked for silver and gold, and the Devil gave it to him. Then he asked for invisibility, which the Devil granted, but without losing sight of him.

> The man was then at his wit's end to think of some third condition that the Devil would be unable to meet. . . . The story goes that at the critical moment, he let fly with a double-barreled fart which went off like a volley of muskets. Then, with great presence of mind he seized his chance and said to the Devil: "Thread me together all those farts and I'm yours."
>
> The Devil tried to thread them; but although he put the eye of his needle to the farts and pulled them through for all he was worth, he could never get to the end of them. And terrified by the horrible din from the farts, which the surrounding echoes had redoubled, and bewildered, indeed frantic, to find that he had been duped, he took to his heels, letting out an infernal creeper which polluted everything round about. Thus was the unhappy man released from the danger that had nearly engulfed him.

Martin Luther, a gourmand of beer and hearty food (perhaps even pumpernickel bread), believed that belching and farting were expressions of a happy belly. Whenever he got sick, he became fearful that the Devil might slip inside his ass and possess his innards, so he'd drink huge tankards of stout beer and gorge himself to flush out any interlopers.

A couple of centuries later, in 1766, German philosopher Immanuel Kant may have been thinking of Luther when he opined in *Dreams of a Visionary*: "If a hypochondriacal wind storms in your bowels, it all depends which direction it takes. Should it go downwards, so a fart comes therefrom, but should it climb upwards, so it is a vision or holy inspiration." Maybe Luther's original revelation was simply a beer fart that went to his head.

But then again, there are many passages in the Bible from which references to flatulence, either figurative or literal, might be construed, for there seems to be a constant blowing of wind over Egypt and Israel throughout the pages of the Old and New Testaments: "And there went forth a wind from the Lord" (Numbers 11:31); "and with his mighty wind shall he shake his hand over the river" (Isaiah 11:15); "and bringeth forth the wind out of his treasures" (Jeremiah 51:16); "A dry wind of the high places in the wilderness toward the daughter of my people, not to fan, nor to cleanse" (Jeremiah 4:11). The Jews' wrathful Jehovah seemed to be farting at his people half the time. Isaiah (Isaiah 63:15) equated the noise from God's stomach to his blessings when he looked heavenward and asked, "Where *is* thy zeal and thy strength, the sounding of thy bowels and of thy mercies toward me? Are they restrained?"

The prophets themselves and their families had a terrible time with gas. Isaiah lamented in a prayer (Isaiah 26:18), "We have been with child, we have been in pain, we have as it were brought forth wind." Job bitched (Job 30:27), "My bowels boiled, and rested not: the days of affliction prevented me." And Jeremiah, always good for a cranky jeremiad, was forever complaining: "I *am* in distress: my bowels are troubled" (Lamentations 1:20); "Mine eyes do fail with tears, my bowels are troubled" (Lamentations 2:11); "My bowels, my bowels! I am pained at my very heart; my heart maketh a noise in me; I cannot hold my peace, because thou hast heard, O my soul, the sound of the trumpet" (Jeremiah 4:19).

In the New Testament, John (John 3:8) pretty much summed

up the whole problem when he observed that "The wind blowest where it listeth, and thou hearest the sound thereof, but canst not tell whence it cometh."

Actually, farts and religion go way, way back together. In *Scatalogic Rites of All Nations*, John G. Bourke wrote,

> It may be well to bear in mind that the heathen idea of the power of a god was entirely different from our own. The deities of the heathen were restricted to their powers and functions. . . . They were not able to cure all diseases, only particular kinds, each god being a specialist; consequently, each was supposed to take charge of a section of the human body. This was the case with the Greeks, Romans, Egyptians, and others. In medieval times, the same rule obtained, only in place of gods, we find saints assigned to these functions.

For example, in Martin Luther's time, the Catholic Church's Saint Erasmus was in charge of "the belly, with the entrayles" and Saint Phiacre the lower tract, including hemorrhoids, "of those especially which grow in the fundament." Earlier, the Romans assigned latrines and sewers to the goddess Cloacina and the bowels and their discharges to Stercutius (shit) and Crepitus (farts), though most scholars believe that Crepitus may have been a caricature and not especially taken seriously.

In the late sixteenth century, Father Juan de Torquemada wrote that ancient Egyptians reveled in farting and other earthy delights: "I assert that they used to *adore* (as St. Clement writes to St. James the Less) stinking and filthy privies and water-closets; and, what is viler and yet more abominable, and an occasion for our tears and not to be borne with or so much as mentioned by name, they adored the noise and wind of the stomach when it expels from itself any cold or flatulence; and other things of the same kind, which, according to the same saint, it would be a shame to name or describe." According to the *Bibliotheca Scatalogica*—an anthology of anonymously written treatises compiled in the nineteenth-century—"Le Pet was an ancient Egyptian goddess; she was the personification of a natural function."

Another nineteenth-century writer, Charles Perry, observed in *A View of the Levant* that "the ancient Pelusiens, a people of lower Egypt, did venerate a Fart, which they worshipped under the symbol of a swelled paunch."

The Moabites assigned the health of their belly and bowels to the deity Bel-Phegor. At Bel-Phegor's altar a supplicant was expected to present his bare ass and make an offering in hopes of keeping himself free of stomach ailments and hemorrhoids. Said Bourke, "The worshipper of Bel-Phegor would offer him the sacrifice of flatulence and excrement, testimonies of the good health for which gratitude was due to the deity." The prophet Isaiah might have been commenting on this practice when, after Jehovah laid waste to the Moabites, he said in chapter 16, verse 11: "Wherefore my bowels shall sound like a harp for Moab, and mine inward parts for [the Moabite city of] Kir-ha'resh."

According to the Parsi author of an ancient work called the *Shapast la Shayast*, the Hebrews hated the heathen god Bel-Phegor because, to them, "The rule is that when one retains a prayer inwardly and wind shall come from below, or wind shall come from the mouth, it is all one"—and the spell of the prayer would be broken because it was "spoken" aloud. Rabbi Solomon Ganzfried, a nineteenth-century Talmudic scholar, wrote that the ancient *Code of Jewish Law* proscribed Jews from looking or aiming their asses in the direction of Jerusalem, the holy city, when they shit or farted. The code further commanded that "If a bad odor went forth from one he is not permitted to engage himself on holy matters until the bad odor disappears; the same law applies to a case where the bad odor went forth from his neighbor. But if he is engaged in the study of the Torah, it is not necessary for him to interrupt his study on account of a bad odor that went forth from his neighbor." Plus, "If one is certain that he could not abstain from letting off wind before finishing the reading of the sh'ma or the prayer, it is preferable that he allows the time limit for the sh'ma and prayer to pass, than praying with an impure body."

Ancient religions of present-day Great Britain paid homage to deities who guarded their backsides, and many of the traditions apparently have survived in games and lore. John Brand, in *Popular*

Antiquities, wrote, "In the stage directions to the old Moralities we often find, 'Here Satan letteth a F—.'" In nineteenth-century London, Brand said, "The porters that plyed at Billingsgate used civilly to entreat and desire each man that passed that way to salute a post that stood there in a vacant place. If he refused to do this, they forthwith laid hold of him, and by main force bouped his [ass] against the post. . . . I believe this was done in memory of some old image that formerly stood there, perhaps of Belius or Belin."

These crude rites are very probably the root of "touch wood" games in which farters are punched or pinched in the arm unless they can run to a tree and touch it first. Such tributes are probably related to the practice near Paris in the fourteenth and fifteenth centuries, related by Victor Hugo in *The Hunchback of Notre Dame*, of requiring prostitutes to make a payment of a fart when they crossed the toll bridge at Montluc.

So the next time you fart, don't say "Excuse me." A simple amen will do.

THOU SHALT NOT DIDDLE THYSELF WITH FARTS

The Catholic Church's venerable Saint Jerome was fearful not only of the sexual joys of marriage, but he was fearful of the joys of farting as well. Born Sophronius Eusebius Hieronymus in Dalmatia (in what is now Croatia) near the middle of the fourth century, Jerome studied in Rome, was baptized by Pope Liberius, and became an ascetic in the year 370. After reportedly receiving a visitation from Jesus Christ during a delirium caused by illness, he prayed and fasted in the isolation of the Syrian desert for four years. At the age of forty-two he returned to Rome and became secretary to Pope Damasus. Jerome later translated the Old Testament from Hebrew to Latin and revised the entire Latin version of the New Testament, creating what is now called the Vulgate, which remained the Catholic Church's official Latin text of the Bible until Pope John Paul II replaced it with the New Vulgate in 1979. Just as important, Jerome began sermonizing on the virtues of sexual abstinence. Perhaps more than anyone else, Jerome was responsible for making the celibacy of nuns and priests an integral philosophy of the Church.

But the man who was later canonized as Saint Jerome had his earthy side. There were rumors that he'd had an affair with Saint Paula, a rich widow who dedicated her life and wealth to the Church. In the year 386, Jerome, Paula, and others of their group settled in Bethlehem, where Paula built three convents for women and a monastery for men and turned the administration of all of them over to Jerome. Ever firm in his doctrine of celibacy, Jerome controlled the day-to-day lives of his nuns. "She who is not married careth for the things of the Lord, that she may be holy in body and in spirit," he wrote in 383. But in his letter "To Furia, on the duty of remaining a widow," dated 394, he especially saw a sexual problem with most foods: "It is good neither to eat flesh nor to drink wine—but with beans also anything that creates wind or lies heavy on the stomach should be rejected. I think that nothing so inflames the body and titillates the genitals as undigested food." In Jerome's words, "*Inpartibus genitalibus titillationes producunt*," which can be translated as "The wind will tickle their pussies."

The idea wasn't new. Two centuries earlier, the Greek philosopher Plutarch wrote, "Why was it ordained that they who were to live chaste should abstain from pulse [peas or beans]? Or rather was it because they should bring empty and slender bodies to their purifications and expiations? For pulse are windy and cause a great deal of excrements that require purging off. Or is it because they excite lechery by reason of their flatulent and windy nature?"

9

MUSICAL FARTS

Trafalgar Rag: "La Fart"!

—palindrome

As a record collector who owns thousands of old blues recordings, many quite explicit, I'm surprised that I've never been able to find a reference to farting in any of them. With all that eatin' pigfeet, drinkin' muddy water, and sleepin' in a hollow log, you'd think there'd be lots of swamp gas. Maybe T-Bone Walker's "Call It Stormy Monday" had a hidden meaning after all. I'll go back and listen to it again. In the meantime, I can tell you about a few hot cracks on wax.

During World War II, RCA Victor's subsidiary label, Bluebird, released a farting record that sold a million and a half copies in the United States and Great Britain. It was "Der Fuehrer's Face" by Spike Jones and His City Slickers, an orchestra noted for parodying pop tunes. The song was originally written by Walt Disney's British-born conductor, Oliver G. Wallace, for a Donald Duck cartoon called "In Nutsy Land," a spoof of the Nazis who were then carving up Europe. Only a few months after the United States joined the war against the Axis powers, Jones's band, fronted by vocalists Carl Grayson and Willie Spicer and armed with rubber razzers to create flabby farting noises, turned Wallace's song into a zany gas attack on Adolf Hitler: "And we'll [*fart! fart!*] right in der Fuehrer's face."

In those days the oral razz—delivered by extending the tongue through partly closed lips and exhaling air to make it vibrate like a fart rumbling through the anus—was innocuously known as "the bird" or "the Bronx cheer." Everybody knew exactly what the razz was supposed to be on Spike Jones's record, but what prude during those dark days was going to be unpatriotic enough to complain about a record glorifying the act of dusting Hitler's mustache with an antifascist fart? "Der Fuehrer's Face," a great morale booster, spent sixteen weeks on *Billboard*'s "Best Selling Records" chart from early October 1942 to February 1943, topping out at number three.

Though it hardly sold as many copies as "Der Fuehrer's Face," perhaps the most infamous farting record of all time is 'The Crepitation Contest.' According to novelty record expert Barret Hansen, better known as Doctor Demento, whose long-running radio show is syndicated on nearly 100 stations all over the United States, "There are at least thirty different editions of 'The Crepitation Contest,' but about twenty are of the same recording, bootlegged and re-bootlegged." Though the original crepitation contest took place in Canada, it was probably recorded in England during or just after World War II and circulated widely on 78-rpm records. "A couple of people have credited its initial distribution to clandestine activities at the Armed Forces Radio Network, whose stations were supplied with disc recorders," says Hansen, "but I've never found anyone who could give me the names of the people who wrote and/or recorded the original, nor when or exactly where it was done." Hansen's studies of various early 78-rpm pressings have convinced him, however, that several editions of the original were made surreptitiously at both the RCA Victor and Columbia record pressing plants.

"The Crepitation Contest's" origins can be found in a fifteenth-century Japanese picture narrative called the "Scroll of Fukutomi," which details the story of an old man named Hidetake, who becomes a popular local entertainer because he can dance to the rhythm of his own farting. His jealous neighbor, Fukutomi, tries to cut in on

Hidetake's glory by learning the old man's craft and challenging him to a farting contest. But Hidetake is no fool. He gives his pupil morning glory seeds, which create diarrhea, and when Fukutomi tries to impress Hidetake's wealthy patrons, he ends up shitting down the back of his legs. (And the moral of the story is: If you've got diarrhea, your ass is not to be trusted with a fart.)

Two centuries later, a 1751 French pamphlet called *L'art de péter*, or *The Art of the Fart*, subtitled, "Essay on the Physical Theory and Method of Farting," told the story of a farting contest between the champions of the armies of Prince Airfart and the Queen of the Amazons. The Amazonian won with a fart that "spilled out and flowed graciously, accompanied by melodious and wondrous sounds without color." But by the end of World War II, in 1945, when Rosie the Riveter was being fired from the factory and directed back home to the kitchen, perhaps the idea of an independent and victorious female farter was too much for men to handle.

In any event, without further ado, I present a transcript of the original "The Crepitation Contest," granddaddy of fart records:

SIDNEY S. BROWN (announcing over crowd sounds): How do you do, ladies and gentlemen, it's our privilege to bring you at this time an eyewitness report of the first international crepitation contest. We are speaking to you from the ringside at the great Maple Leaf Auditorium, which is packed to the rafters with spectators, eager and curious. For the benefit of my listeners who are not acquainted with the facts relating to this event, it might be well to describe the two contestants. Lord Windesmere from Wopping Foghole in Devonshire is of course the champion of the British Empire. The challenger is Paul Boomer, native son of Australia, who I understand worked his way to Canada in the crew of an ocean freighter carrying a load of Melbourne cabbage upon which, so it is stated, Boomer trains exclusively. [*Crowd reacts.*] Ah, I see now there's a bit of flurry around Lord Windesmere's entrance, and yes, here he comes, Lord Windesmere. I'll see if I can get him to come to the microphone to say a few words.

Joe, see if you can get his lordship to come over here for a
minute. Tell him it's for the radio.

JOE: OK, I'll get him for you.

SIDNEY: Thanks. Well, our Lord Windesmere appears to be
in good spirits, he's smiling and chatting, thrown about him
is a beautiful silk dressing gown of purple velvet upon which
I imagine to be the coat of arms of the house of Windesmere.
It's a beautiful thing—ah, good boy, Joe. Ah, in just a minute,
ladies and gentlemen, I think we're going to have his lordship
himself come to the microphone and say a few words—ah,
right over here please, right over here. Yes, right here, yes,
yes, folks, here he is, right in the microphone, the champion
himself, Lord Windesmere. Your Highness, how did you
come to take an interest in this unusual art?

WINDESMERE (very English): Well, I suppose you could say it
all started over Lady Windesmere's fan.

SIDNEY: I see.

WINDESMERE: Yes, I noticed she was constantly waving this
fan in front of her face, so I asked her why in deuce she did
it. And so she retorted that if I insisted on constantly crepitating, she had to fan away in pure self defense, you see. So, my
friends were drawn into the controversy and persuaded me to
capitalize on my proficiency, and sort of going for it and all
that. That's all.

SIDNEY: Thank you very much, Your Majesty, thank you,
and good luck to you. That was Lord Windesmere, a champion crepper here at the—[crowd noises]. Oh, and here's the
challenger, yes, Paul Boomer from Australia. Paul, over here
please! Please, ask Mr. Boomer to come over here, please!
The radio, we want to speak on the radio. Just a moment,
ladies and gentlemen, I think we'll have Paul Boomer for you
right away. Yes, here he comes. His attendant has just pointed us out, ah howdy, Paul. Ha-ha. He just raises his hand in
greeting and starts walking over to the microphone. And

here, ladies and gentlemen, is Mr. Paul Boomer. Will you say hello to our audience, Mr. Boomer?

BOOMER (in an exaggerated Aussie accent): Hello, Canada.

SIDNEY: Now tell me, sir, when did you first realize that you were proficient enough to take a shot at the Empire championship?

BOOMER: Well, ever since I was a little nipper I liked to fart. I remember I used to make me mother and father laugh their bleedin' 'eads off when I used to let one go in church during the announcement of the ladies' aid.

SIDNEY: Excuse me, Mr. Boomer, on the radio we call it crepitating.

BOOMER: Now look here, cobber, what I always says is, a fart's a fart, whether you raise up on one cheek and sneak, or whether you give it a full blast like I do.

SIDNEY: Very well, as long as the CBC sees no objection, I personally find the four-letter word much easier to say and more descriptive than the longer, more academic *crepitating*.

BOOMER: Thank you. And I'd like to say . . . [*bell sounds*].

SIDNEY: And there's the bell. Thank you, Mr. Boomer, and good luck. Paul Boomer hurries off to the center of the arena to meet the champion and to receive instructions. Now the house lights are dimming and the great flood of high-powered electric lights cascade down onto the center of this great arena where stands, in simple eloquence, the farting post. The farting post is about four feet high and decorated in red, white, and blue bunting up to about nine inches from the top. The bare top section is worn smooth by the grip of many hands in previous contests. And now it appears that Paul Boomer is to be the first at the post. That, I believe, is customary for the challenger to make the first effort. Yes, Paul Boomer takes off his dressing gown and strides to the farting post. He grips it firmly around the top and flexes his knees.

The signal to commence has not yet been given so we may

assume these are just preliminaries. I think I have time to describe Mr. Boomer's outfit. He's stripped from the waist up and wears tight-fitting trunks of powder blue trimmed with scarlet. These trunks are similar to those worn by wrestlers, with one important difference. There's a hole about six inches in back entirely removed from the seat. This of course has been done for obvious reasons. This symmetric aperture is called the *finesse de breeze*, roughly translated meaning the "zephyr window." Mr. Boomer's *finesse de breeze* has a scarlet trim around its perimeter giving a very provocative air to this genial Australian backside. [*A fartlike horn blares.*] And there goes the signal to commence. You might have heard it over the microphone, a blast on the medieval brown Sousaspiegel, the traditional woodwind instrument associated with this sport for centuries.

And now a hush falls on the vast throng as Boomer walks slowly, deliberately to the farting post. He's exuding confidence and he gives one last all-encompassing grin to the tense audience as he grips the farting post between a pair of hands that look as though they could splinter the farting post. Now he flexes his knees, much in the manner of a boxer. He seems to be concentrating on the very top of the farting post. You can hear a pin drop, and here it comes [*three short snorts*]. Oh, a beauty, a beauty, I think it was a triple flutter blast. Yes, that's what the judge signals, a triple flutter blast. That gives him twenty-five points right off the bat [*three more short farts*]. And another of the same, and another twenty-five points [*one snip of a fart*]. That's followed by one. . . . [*more short farts*] no, two, I beg your pardon, three fudgy farts in rapid succession. It's amazing how this man can change pace and style by a slight simple shifting of his buttock area. He's still gripping the post in complete concentration. Boomer now has a score of sixty-five, those last three fudgy farts at five points apiece, adding fifteen to his previous score. And now here's something coming up [*a long, ripping fart*], a flooper, a flooper, a perfectly executed flooper. What's that? I'm sorry, ladies and gentlemen, that was a follow-up flooper, a follow-up flooper, the second time in the history of this sport that a follow-up flooper has been achieved in open competition. The only other time, I believe, was during the world series held in Europe in 1783. During the course of that series Francois Foof, the famous French farter, after leaving a follow-up flooper, defeated Sandy McWind, his Scottish opponent by only one bloop, and then dropped dead. As you know, since then, in honor of Messr. Foof, the bloop had been dropped from northern competition. And now the score is 105 for Boomer. A flooper of course counts ten points, but a follow-up flooper, a very difficult maneuver, gives forty points. Well, it's certainly been a whirlwind session. I think that Paul Boomer is about played out, or blown out as they say [*two more farts*]. What am I saying? And he's not through yet, apparently. Wait a minute, here comes . . . [*a tiny fart*]. A freep! Oh oh, little freep, worth only two points, and very dangerous [*poot!*]. And another. [*poot!*] And another freep. Well, not bad [*poot!*]. Well, he's . . . [*laughter*]. Well, he's certainly putting up a fighting finish, four freeps, a very hazardous fart because of the danger of flotching, but giving him eight very valuable points. [*The crowd cheers.*] And there, he throws up his hands, he throws up his hands as a signal that he's finished, and the crowd gives him a tremendous ovation. He's sitting down, looking a little pale, a little wan perhaps, but smiling, smiling happily at the crowd. This man has a definite charm about him that has endeared him to all except the most rabid Windesmere fan. And, wait a minute. . . .

REFEREE (shouting): Paul Boomer, one hundred and twenty-three points!

SIDNEY (above the crowd's roar): Did you hear that? Paul

Boomer, a hundred and twenty-three points, a world's record, beating Lord Windesmere's previous world mark of one hundred nineteen by four points. Paul Boomer this moment is the world's champion, but for how long we don't know because Lord Windesmere might take it right back again.

And here's His Lordship now walking up to the post apparently not in the least disconcerted by the brilliant performance of the challenger. He's outfitted a little differently from Paul Boomer. He has purple tights, full-length tights, and around the *finesse de breeze*—you remember, the hole cut out from the center of his seat—around this is a fringe of little gold tassels about four inches long. This no doubt is some decoration affected by . . . just a moment! Seems to be some sort of dispute here. Paul Boomer and his seconds are on their feet and seem to be arguing with the judges and pointing to the fringe on the champion's posterior. Oh, I see, Paul Boomer is claiming that the fringe might add a whistle or some other sound to Lord Windesmere's efforts and so increase their value. And after all, in a close free-fart contest like this every little advantage must be jealously watched. The judges appear to be in agreement with Paul Boomer, and they direct the champion to remove the fringe. He doesn't like the decision very much, and the crowd is getting . . . the crowd is getting resentful, they think he should be a better sport about it, and I agree with them. He seems to have decided that he's got to give in, and he rips off the fringe and flings it to the ground. Then he walks over to where Boomer's sitting and turns his back, puts his hands on his hips and [*the ripping sound of a fart*] oh, oh, he leans a freep right in poor Boomer's face! The crowd gets a kick out of this. As you know, a freep is a very low score, only two points, but to throw one away just in a gesture of defiance demonstrates the spirit of dashing recklessness which has made the Englishman the champion that he is.

He's smiling distinctly now as he returns to the center of

the arena. He nods to the judge to show he's ready and he—hello, what's this? He's not going to use the farting post. Lord Windesmere the champion, in a final gesture of contempt, scorns the use of the farting post. Well, this is developing into a bit of a grudge contest. He has his hands on his hips, he's slightly bent and [*fart*]—a sizzler, his first attempt [*fart*]—and another one, two in a row [*fart*], and another one, a third. Three sizzlers in a row, a tremendous effort, sixty points in his first thirty seconds . . . [*four short blasts*] and one, two, three, four—four fudgies, four fragrant fudgies in rapid succession. It's a pleasure to see the ease and comfort with which His Lordship leaves his farts. Perfect technique. And now his score is eighty points, eighty points in the first thirty seconds at the post. And he's getting ready again, hands on hips, a little bit red in the face, acting strange [*flubbery sound*]—oh, something there, wait a minute, something's wrong, his attendants running to him, he's in some kind of distress! I see, yes, the judge's signal, it was a plotcher. Oh, hard luck, your lordship, hard luck. The champion left a very bad plotcher and will be penalized fifteen points. That puts him back to sixty-five points, fifty-nine short of the one hundred twenty-four he needs to retain his championship.

He's all set again and seems to be straining a little more cautiously, and here is [*a very long, winding fart*]—a thunders break, oh, a beautiful bit of windbreaking virtuosity, a most difficult, a most difficult fart to perform without plotching. This man has wonderful control, and the crowd are really warming up to him. That thunders break counts thirty points, and it takes Lord Windesmere up to ninety-five points. It's getting very tense now, and here it is, here is the next one [*three short whiny blasts*]—a trill blow, a trill blow, ten points—[*a savage blast*] followed by a resounding single flutter blast, I think that is. Yes, the judges proclaim that to be a single flutter blast, a lovely change of pace there, and now the excitement is growing unbearable as the champion takes a step away from the post, and his score is one hundred twenty, just three points short. If he gets one more fudgy or two small freeps, it's all over but the shouting and the challenger will have to return to Australia with his shattered hopes. I think everyone's heart aches for poor Boomer. He's really a great guy.

Windesmere steps up to the post again and looks very confident as he gets ready for the killing. And here it comes [*a tiny fart*]—a freep, that's two more points, a little small freep was all it was, two points, and now it's back to the oval and just one more of those little freeps, those little two-point freeps, and the contest will be over. It seems as though His Lordship was deliberately tormenting Boomer by daring, but Boomer is smiling. It's a forced smile, but he's sitting there, trying hard to take it like the grand sportsman that he is, but he can see defeat standing ready to sweep away his dreams at almost any instant.

And now Lord Windesmere steps forward and, hello, hello, he's going to use the farting post for this final effort, it seems. He flexes his knees. It looks as though he's going to try for a high-scoring effort for a whirlwind finish. Perhaps another sizzler. And now he's trying very hard, the veins are starting out on his forehead, and even the trickle of perspiration venturing down his temple seems to hesitate, so that this mighty last effort should have undivided attention. Now a projection of a smile from the champion, he seems to decide just what treatment he's going to give this final bid. The audience almost to a man is on its feet, breathless and tense. He closes his eyes. A look of pure ecstasy on his face. [*A distorted sound*] Ohhhh, he *shit*! [*The crowd reacts.*] The champion is disqualified!

Now ladies and gentlemen, as a special service feature we have brought you direct from the ringside of the Maple Leaf Auditorium a blow by blow description of the first crepitation contest held under international auspices. This broadcast replaces midweek meditations usually held at this time. Your narrator, Sidney S. Brown.

There it is, "The Crepitation Contest" in its original form. This classic remains available on CD and cassette. One place to find it is the Fart Mart at www.farts.com/mart.htm, or by phone at 1-900-ALL-FART.

Over the next three decades, small-time entrepreneurs put out several updated recordings of "The Crepitation Contest." Doctor Demento's favorite is "The Glick Version," a faithful remake of the original script, with only subtle changes, released on a ten-inch LP (Glick GLK-101) from the Glick Record Company in Oak Park, Illinois, in the 1960s. "The recording is clearer and the farts are more spectacular in sound," says Demento. "Of course I had to edit out the words fart and shit for airplay when I played it in the 1970s. I also have a tape of some outtakes from this recording in which the narrator breaks up and says, 'I can't go through with this' or something like that, but not even that version identifies him." The narrator, incidentally, begins this updated version by calling it the "trepidation" contest.

Though most versions of "The Crepitation Contest" use roughly the same script, they often vary in location and use different names for both the contestants and the farts. Producer Jay Miller of Crowley, Louisiana, who sometimes specialized in KKK recordings, released a race-baiting farting contest on two 45-rpm singles on the Ruff label (2000 and 2001), "rescribed" in the minstrel tradition by a caricature of a pompous black man reminiscent of the Kingfish from *Amos & Andy*. "Now I'se speakin' to ya, live and di-rect from ringside at beautiful Abraham Arena," where the "crepitatin' cham-peen of da world are Windy H. Fartenberry, an old tongue-tied boy from Rectum Blowhole a-way down in Mississippi." Challenging Windy is Mr. Oober Goober Boomer from Birmingham, Alabama, who "done eat-up and trained-up his own self in da art of crepitatin' exclusively" by feasting on cabbage and sweet potatoes on a freighter running between Birmingham and the Belgian Congo. Oober Goober brags to the announcer, "I likes to fart!" In the end, as Windy H. Fartenberry grunts and groans in a desperate last attempt to retain his title, the narrator makes a sudden shocked announcement: "Holy mackerel, he *crapped!* Da cham-peen crapped out here."

A 45-rpm single (SL90613) from Outhouse Records in Cincinnati, Ohio, set the "farting tournament" in Luke Tillman's tobacco warehouse somewhere in the South (broadcast over radio station WIND, in conjunction with the International Farters Association of America). The contest is narrated in an amiable drawl by a Kentuckian named Clarence Loos—the only person on any of the subsequent farting contest records who actually owned up to it. The champion is one Thelan Colon; his challenger is Elmer Adkins from Titusville, Tennessee. The farting post is located in the middle of a ring, in which the two men square off wearing terry cloth robes emblazoned with the emblem of the IFAA.

Whoever put this record together decided that the names of the various farts needed updating. The "flutter blast" became the "Tennessee weeper" (twenty-five points), the "fudgy" was a "fuzzy fart" (five points), and the amazing "follow-up flooper" was now the "follow-up Birmingham blunderbuss" (thirty points). The dangerous but unimpressive "freep" evolved into the "Fort Campbell fluke" (two points).

As in the original contest, it all comes down to one fart the champ needs to keep his title. "If he can jest make this one more little fuzzy, maybe, or jest a fluke, he'll be tall hog at the trough tonight," Loos announces. Then comes a long, dribbling, drabbling thing, and Loos disqualifies him: "He shee-*it*!"

Though "The Crepitation Contest" remains Barret Hansen's favorite, he has played other farting records on *The Doctor Demento Radio Show*. They include:

- "Blowing Off" by the Goodies, on Island Records, from the mid-1970s.
- "Armpit Farts" by Zilch Fletcher.
- "Serenade to a Maid" by Teddy Powell and His Orchestra, a 1940s record featuring the lyric: "If I were as high as a bird in the sky, I'd look down at you and go [farting sound]."

- "I'm a Fool for Beans" by the Fletcher Peck Trio, on Decca Records, from 1952 (which has no vocal reference to farting in the lyric, but does showcase a prominent tuba in the band).
- "Somebody Farted," a twelve-inch single by Bobby Jimmy and the Critters, a 1980s novelty rap act from Los Angeles. Released on Profile Records, this song dented *Billboard*'s R&B chart. Bobby Jimmy, whose real name is Russ Parr, also recorded a song called "Big Butt," which has a verse that leads the listener to believe he's going to say *fart*, but he always says something else. Both songs, says Demento, were popular on his show.

In 1997 Bobby Jimmy's accusation was finally answered with "I Farted," a song by a New Jersey P-funk R&B group named Freakwincey. Recorded for a British label called Rephlex, "I Farted" (CAT 060) resounds with plenty of flatulent rejoinders, available in a video mix, a radio mix, and a "trumpapella" mix on either CD or a twelve-inch EP.

One record that Doctor Demento has never played is a hard-to-find 1962 album called *Mark Twain's 1601* (see chapter 7). The West Point edition of Twain's flatulent one-act play is read by one Richard Dyer-Bennet, sounding very much like a drama professor; he released the album on his own Dyer-Bennet label, which may account for its rarity.

In 1978 a mysterious company, Clack, Inc., released a seven-inch, $33\frac{1}{3}$-rpm single on Uranus Records called "The Longest Fart in the World," but the prodigious flatus did not sound realistic. It should have been titled "The World's Longest Bronx Cheer." (However, the flipside, "The Biggest Bowel Movement Bar None," is a masterpiece of grunting, shitting, and farting on the toilet. Jeff Daniels's much-touted, laxative-induced crap in the 1995 film *Dumb and Dumber* sounds suspiciously like Clack's "The Biggest Bowel Movement Bar None," with perhaps some overdubbing from other sources.)

In 1992 the band Spinal Tap, spinning off from their earlier film spoof *This Is Spinal Tap*, recorded an album called *Break Like the Wind*, whose title sounds as flatulent as the band's music, but the enclosed song of the same name only hints at its cryptic meaning: "And will our voices be heard, or will they break like the wind? . . . Swearing to heaven, is this a promise we keep, or one we break like the wind? . . . And will our hearts still beat on, or will they break like the wind?" There's no overt farting, but the lyrics are clever. Another song on the album, "Stinking Up the Great Outdoors," likewise promises more than it delivers.

In 1997 Atlantic Records released Bob Rivers's *Best of Twisted Tunes*, Vol. 1, featuring a hilarious take on the truly flatulent Barbra Streisand and Neil Diamond snoozer, "You Don't Bring Me Flowers." Called "You Don't Smell Like Flowers," the song—crooned by Streisand and Diamond soundalikes—lists all the problems that intimate couples must deal with sooner or later, including blasting off farts in each other's presence.

Finally, perhaps the most inventive fart recording of all time is an unreleased performance called "Butt Flute," by John Tush. A perfect example of *arse musica*, it can be heard occasionally on Howard Stern's radio show, along with a similar treatment of the 1958 instrumental tune, "Tequila." Anyone who remembers the singing dogs yelping "Jingle Bells" will appreciate a song composed of various computer-sampled farts combining to provide the beats, the melody, and the harmony all at once. "Butt Flute" is the ultimate fart record: a kind of a cappella doo-wop performance that only hints at the possibilities. (For Howard Stern's own musical fart performance to the tune of "Wipe Out" on network television, see chapter 10.)

Lest you think that musical farting is a modern curse, consider that several classical composers wrote flatulence into some of their works. I could easily direct you to Richard Strauss's bassoon-heavy *Till Eulenspiegel's Merry Pranks* and Hector Berlioz's *Symphonie Fantastique*, but perhaps the worst offender was that boy wonder Mozart, who typically favored the orchestra's wind section.

Wolfgang Amadeus Mozart (1756-1791) lived for only thirty-five years, but he created hundreds of concertos, symphonies, operas, and smaller pieces—most of which are still admired the world over. Some of the Austrian composer's theatrical works—

including *Don Giovanni*, *Der Fliedermaus*, *The Marriage of Figaro*, and *The Magic Flute*—continue to captivate audiences, and his body of liturgical music, including the Requiem Mass in D minor, has become nearly sacred. Along with Beethoven and Bach, Mozart is considered to be one of the greatest musical geniuses of all time.

But what the general public generally didn't know until the popularity of the play *Amadeus* and the 1984 Academy Award–winning film it inspired, was that Mozart had a strong coprophilic streak. He often joked about eating shit, licking or smelling assholes, and of course letting farts. Apparently this toilet humor ran in the family. His mother, Maria Anna Mozart, wrote the following to her husband, Leopold, on September 9, 1777: "Keep well, my love. Into your mouth your arse you'll shove. I wish you good-night, my dear, but first shit in your bed and make it burst." These seem to be common German idioms whose meanings aren't quite clear in translation.

That mother and son shared scatological intimacies was evident in a prose poem that Wolfgang Mozart, visiting in Worms, composed for her in a January 31, 1778, letter:

> Oh, mother mine! Butter is fine. Praise and thanks be to
> Him, we're alive and full of vim. Through the world we dash,
> though we're rather short of cash. But we don't find this pro-
> voking, and none of us are choking. Besides, to people I'm
> tied who carry their muck inside, and let it out if they are
> able, both before and after table. At night of farts there is no
> lack, which are let off, forsooth, with a powerful crack. The
> king of farts came yesterday, whose farts smelt sweeter than
> the may [like honey]. His voice, however, was no treat, and
> he himself was in a heat. Well, now we've been over a week
> away, and we've been shitting every day. . . . With our shit-
> ting, God we cannot hurt, and least of all if we bite the dirt.
> We are honest birds, all of a feather, we have *summa sum-
> marum* eight eyes together, not counting those on which we

sit. But now I really must rest a bit from rhythming. Yet this
I must add, that on Monday I'll have the honor, egad, to
embrace you and kiss your hands so fair. But first in my
pants I'll shit, I swear.

Mozart saved his best stuff for his attractive young cousin,
Maria Anna Thekla, whom he fondly called Basle. Several letters he
wrote to her in Augsburg have survived. In the first one, written on
November 5, 1777, Mozart peppered his passages with nonsense,
inside jokes, and insults, such as "I shit on your nose and it will run
down your chin." Further on, he interrupts the flow of his quill
with a fart, and a description: "Why yes, muck, I know, see and
smell you . . . and . . . what is that?—Is it possible . . . Ye gods!—
Can I believe these ears of mine? Yes indeed, it is so—what a long
melancholy note." Several lines later he tells the sweet girl,

> As I was doing my best to write this letter, I heard something
> on the street. I stopped writing—I got up—went to the win-
> dow . . . the sound ceased. I sat down again, started off again
> to write—but I had hardly written ten words when again I
> heard something. I got up again—as I did, I again heard a
> sound, this time quite faint—but I seemed to smell something
> slightly burnt—and wherever I went, it smelt. When I looked
> out of the window, the smell disappeared. When I looked
> back into the room, I again noticed it. In the end, Mamma
> said to me: "I bet that you have let one off." "I don't think
> so, Mamma," I replied. "Well, I am certain that you have,"
> she insisted. Well, I thought, "Let's see," put my finger to my
> arse and then to my nose and—*Ecce, provatum est*. Mamma
> was right after all.

In another letter to Fraulein Thekla a week later, Mozart
wrote, "I've been shitting, so 'tis said, nigh twenty-two years
through the same old hole, which is not yet frayed one whit, though
I've used it daily to shit. . . ." And to fart, one must presume,
although in yet another letter to Basle he signed himself, "W. A.

Mozart, who shits without a fart." On December 3, 1777, he implored her: "Please give a whole arseful of greetings from us both to all our good friends." Nearly three months later, on February 28, 1778, Mozart asked his cousin if she was mad at him over some slight, and, if so, was she ready to make peace? "If not," he wrote, "I swear I'll let off one behind." Toward the end of that year, December 23, he asked Basle to join him, phrasing the invitation in a prose rhyme: "So come for a bit or else I'll shit. If you do, this high and mighty person will think you very kind, will give you a smack behind, will kiss your hands, my dear, shoot off a gun in the rear, embrace you warmly, mind, and wash your front and your behind, pay you all his debts to the uttermost, and shoot off one with a rousing note, perhaps even let something drop from his boat."

Brigid Brophy, in her book *Mozart the Dramatist*, remarked that he used "the explosion of air from brass instruments in a comic sense unmistakably parallel to his comic letters." These bursts are especially pronounced in the overtures to his operas. However, during the numerous times Mozart conducted the orchestrations of his works, there is no record whatsoever of him asking, "Is there a *fliedermaus* in here?" or provoking any of his musicians to "pull my baton." Still, you have to wonder where he got the inspiration for *The Magic Flute*.

SALVADOR DALI'S FARTS COULD ALMOST WILT A POCKET WATCH

The popular German magazine *Der Spiegel* reported that during the final days of his life, the internationally famous Spanish surrealist painter Salvador Dali spent a great deal of time philosophizing about his last fart (which finally arrived in 1989).

Dali had a lifelong fascination with farts. "The Crepitation Contest" record was a favorite of his; so was a book he owned called *The Art of Farting* by Count Trumpet, which Dali included as a chapter in his autobiography, *Diary of a Genius*—though it has been expunged from most editions. *The Art of Farting* contained a facetious seventeenth-century Spanish pamphlet called *The Benefit of Farting Explain'd*, written under the pseudonym Don Fartinando "and translated into English at the Request, and for the Use of the Lady Damp-fart of Her-Fart-Shire by Obediah Fizzle, Groom of the stool to the Princess of Arsmimini in Sardinia."

In his diary, dated July 3, 1952, Salvador Dali remembered: "I had an aunt who was horrified by everything scatological. The very idea that she might break wind filled her eyes with tears. She staked her honor on the fact that she had never farted in her life. Today I consider her achievement less impressive than I used to." Later that month, July 29, he remarked upon only one event that day: "Because of a very long fart, really a very long and, let us be frank, melodious one, that I produced when I woke up, I was reminded of Michel de Montaigne. This author reports that Saint Augustine was a famous farter who succeeded in playing entire scores."

(Actually, Montaigne had simply written: "To show the limitless authority of our wills, Saint Augustine cites the example of a man who could make his behind produce farts whenever he would." What St. Augustine had actually written, circa A.D. 420, was: "Some have such command of their bowels, that they can break wind continuously at pleasure, so as to produce the effect of singing." It seems that when the subject is farting, exaggeration takes over.)

Dali later might have been riffing on that same inspirational flatus when he said, "I hardly fart anymore, and only on awakening, very melodiously. This morning, I dedicated my fart to St. Augustine, prince of petomanes, for I am in my mystical phase."

10
GONE WITH THE WIND

He made his blazing saddle a torch
to light the way!

—*Frankie Laine, singing the Oscar-nominated*
theme song to Mel Brooks's Blazing Saddles

Dateline Hollywood: In an industry where a bad movie is called a "stinker," it seems only proper that farting has finally become boffo box office. Nearly every nineties comedy film has had at least one gratuitous fart scene, and lowbrow comedians load up their movies with flatulence as a respite from the otherwise lack of funny. TV sitcoms also have gotten in on the act and joined Tinseltown's cutting-cheese edge.

We can credit (or blame) the breakdown of nearly every other media taboo over the past twenty-five years for this flurry of cinematic crepitation. But equally significant is a shift in Hollywood's economics and demographics. As film studios pump higher budgets into their projects and therefore require blockbusters to recoup their investments, they tailor their product for their most reliable audience: adolescent males, domestic and foreign. And the two mainstays certain to appeal to young men in all parts of the world are fast, gory action and gross body humor. Similarly, TV producers floundering in a glutted sitcom market—thanks in part to the addition of three junior networks—have found that a good fart is worth a dozen of the usual verbal put-downs. There's been enough gaseous humor wafting off the screen that a couple of years ago *New York Times* columnist Michiko Kakutani felt prompted to ask, "When did we become a nation of twelve-year-olds?"

It wasn't always so. Though Bing Crosby and Bob Hope could get away with planting a whoopee cushion in Anthony Quinn's chair in a World War II-era comedy called *Road to Morocco*, Hollywood generally allowed neither the hint of a scent nor a mimicry of a fart. Its guardian of decency was the William Hays Office, which had been around since the early twenties but didn't formally take control of studio morality and good taste until 1934, following an uproar over Mae West's mildly ribald films. The Hays Office's canon of deportment was the Motion Picture Production Code—more familiarly called the "Don'ts and Be Carefuls." Under the Code, all intimations of blasphemy (religious disrespect), obscenity (sex), and vulgarity (other bodily functions) were duly expunged. "The treatment of low, disgusting, unpleasant . . . subjects should be guided always by the dictates of good taste and proper regard for the sensibilities of the audience," said the Code.

Those sensibilities were deemed to be very delicate. For example, in 1936 Joe Breen of the Hays Office complained to United Artists about Charlie Chaplin's *Modern Times*: "We respectfully urge upon you the following eliminations," one being "the business of the stomach rumbling on the part of the minister's wife and Charlie." In 1941, after screening W. C. Fields's *Never Give a Sucker an Even Break*, Breen warned Universal Pictures, "The word 'stinker' will be deleted by some [state] censor boards. Also the word 'stinkeroo,'" and he insisted that "The business of Fields scratching the match on the seat of the man's pants will have to be handled carefully." Breen must have missed Fields's opening scene, in which a fruit seller shouts "raspberries" while a tire on his truck makes a razzbery sound, because ten years later the producers of *Bedtime for Bonzo*, a film starring Ronald Reagan and a chimpanzee, were told that "'Razzberry' is on the [Motion Picture Association of America's] list of unacceptable words and expressions and [can] not be approved."

In 1968 the motion picture industry scuttled the Hays Office after several state courts declared the Motion Picture Production Code unconstitutional, and replaced it with the Classification and Ratings Administration, whose job was to assign ratings to films according to their sexual content, level of violence, and to a lesser extent, amount and degree of vulgarity.

Three years later, in 1971, the CRA gave an X rating to a disjointed, rather salacious Italian-French production of Geoffrey Chaucer's *Canterbury Tales*, filmed in England with mostly British non-actors by controversial Italian director Pier Paolo Pasolini. Though he included plenty of onscreen debauchery, Pasolini especially lingered on Chaucer's two major fart scenes (see chapter 5). In "The Miller's Tale" Pasolini made sure poor Absolon got two very loud and lusty farts in his face. And though the director sharply abridged "The Summoner's Tale," in which the bedridden old man, Thomas, farts (also very loudly) into the hand of the unctious Friar John, he borrowed the summoner's prologue, in which the Canterbury pilgrim describes how 20,000 friars swarmed out of Satan's ass, and tagged it on the end of the story. But instead of mere swarming, Pasolini showed them being endlessly shitted and farted from the Devil's anus like so much diarrhea. The film did well in Europe, but it was restricted to a handful of art houses and porno palaces when it arrived in America in 1972.

It would take another couple of years before Hollywood studios decided to cut to the cheese. The film was Mel Brooks's

---

At a power lunch at The Ivy in Beverly Hills, three studio executives are busily trying to impress each other.

Suddenly a beeper goes off. One of the executives presses the gold medallion hanging around his neck to his ear and speaks briefly into his Rolex watch. After he hangs up, he says, "This is my new experimental cell phone."

Another beeper goes off. The second hotshot starts talking to nobody in particular. After he finishes he says, "The latest technology. My speaker's implanted in my ear and the cap of my front tooth is a microphone."

The third hotshot responds by blasting a fart that nearly shakes the Perrier bottles off the table. He stands up and heads toward the bathroom. "Pardon me, fellas," he says, "but I'm ready to receive a fax!"

Blazing Saddles, a 1974 parody of Western movies that presented an indelible scene of cowpokes sitting around a prairie campfire, eating their beans and relentlessly spooking the horses with a barrage of farting that sounds like the gunfight at the O.K. Corral. What made this fireside serenade so funny was that filmmakers had been showing cowboys scarfing down beans since the silent era, yet nobody had ever hinted at the natural result of this diet. "I mean, you can't eat so many beans without some noise happening there," Mel Brooks said at the time. Brooks, whose own character in the film is called Governor William J. Le Petomane, considered the campfire scene his funniest gag, for even the film's title (changed from *Black Bart* shortly before its release) was a reference to heated farting on horseback.

In fact, though Warner Brothers trimmed the film by at least thirty minutes, Brooks adamantly refused to let them tamper with his farting scene, because its very length was critical to its comic timing. As he would tell *Playboy* a year later, "With the first fart, a slight shudder goes through the [film audience] and you can hear a gasp from the people who are just a little more sensitive. With the next series of three or four farts, titters begin to escape from mouths. The fifth or sixth fart evokes a flat-out laugh from a third of the audience. By the time the *sixteenth* fart rolls around, the entire audience is in a state of hysterical convulsions."

The humor, farts and all, of *Blazing Saddles* became the subject of countless editorials. "The non-stop vulgarity—in a movie that . . . features a symphony of flatulence from beans-eating cowhands—can make one yearn to come up for air," complained *The New York Times*'s Peter Schjeldahl. Another *Times* writer, Urjo Kareda, began an editorial with: "Every society has its unspoken taboos. They linger in the twilight of public consciousness until something called bad taste brings them into the open"—then he tore into *Blazing Saddles* and a couple of other new films. Clearly *Blazing Saddles*' fartings and other vulgarities had kicked up some serious dust.

Despite all the noise, however, the word *fart* itself is never spoken in *Blazing Saddles*. (Straw boss Slim Pickens merely waves his hat in the air and tells the cowboys, "You've had enough.") It did appear as an insult that same year in a British film, *Monty Python and the Holy Grail*, when John Cleese stands on the top of a fort and shouts down to a troupe of errant knights, "I fart in your general direction!" But the line is a throwaway, lost in the unrelenting anarchy of the film's humor.

It would take another six years before the word became wind in America. In Floyd Mutrex's *The Hollywood Knights*, a 1980 slapstick knockoff of George Lucas's *American Graffiti*, comic Robert Wuhl is a goofy teenage character named Newcomb Turk who can fart at will. During a rally at the Beverly Hills High School auditorium, Wuhl leaps upon the stage and sings "Nel Blu Dipinto Di Blu"—better known as "Volare"—as a call-and-response number; to answer each vocal line he puts the microphone between his legs and blows rich, raucous *flati* as if he'd spent the day eating pinto beans.

One member of the audience runs outside and tells police, "Officers, there's a guy in there in a major domo outfit, *farting*!"

The cops look at each other. "*Farting*?"

"Yes, *farting*!"

There it was. Say a word three times and it's yours forever. Now that the spoken fart was out in the open, all that remained was a cinematic duplication of a fart's scent.

Enter cult filmmaker John Waters, who by 1981 was shooting his first Hollywood movie, *Polyester*. Already infamous for bringing really bad taste—like eating dog shit—to celluloid, Waters decided to pay the tasteless fart special homage. *Polyester* was a satire of modern America's fetish for cleanliness. Transvestite actor Divine, playing suburban housewife Francine Fishpaw, spends much of the film spritzing aerosol fresheners throughout the overdecorated rooms of her upscale suburban house, ignoring her husband's assertion that "This whole world stinks, Francine, so get used to it."

The gimmick Waters devised to promote *Polyester* was an olfactory stimulant called Odorama. Unlike Aroma-Rama and Smell-O-Vision, two systems that atomized various fragrances into theaters in 1959 and 1960 during the screenings of *Behind the*

Great Wall and *Scent of Mystery*, respectively, Odorama was strictly low-budget and low-tech: a five-by-twelve cardboard card with ten numbers printed on pink circles. Each customer picked up an Odorama card along with his ticket at the box office on his way in. During ten separate scenes, a number flashed upon the screen, alerting the audience that it was time to scratch the corresponding number on the card with a coin or thumbnail to activate the chemically created smell underneath.

In a prologue to the story, Odorama is solemnly explained by Dr. Arnold Quackenshaw, standing in a laboratory classroom in front of a chart of a large nose. There's an ominous tinge in his voice as he warns the audience, "You may experience some odors that will shock you!"

Polyester's most memorable scene comes when Divine, lying in bed with her husband, slips a quiet pajama cough under the covers and delicately tries to wave it away. Suddenly the number 2 begins flashing on the screen as her husband answers her with a horrendous fart that puffs up the sheets. The audiences at the original performances groaned *en masse*, but a daring few scratched number 2 on their Odorama cards to catch a whiff of ersatz flatus. Even today, when I recount that treasured moment, it still brings tears to my eyes. (When *Polyester* was reissued on laser disc in the early nineties, a limited-edition replica of the Odorama card was included.)

Meanwhile, in 1981, Tinseltown was taming down the fart, giving it a more genteel treatment in the popular Dudley Moore-Liza Minnelli comedy *Arthur*, which contains a running gag about Moore's nutty grandmother (Geraldine Fitzgerald) whacking at her dog with a newspaper whenever she farts. The poor animal cringes the moment it hears her let one off.

Comic Rodney Dangerfield (who in the 1980 comedy *Caddyshack* had apologized for a low fart with an "Oops, I stepped on a duck!") returned flatulence to its rightfully rude place in the 1986 comedy *Back to School*, the story of a crude, self-made millionaire helping his son through college by enrolling alongside him. Tugging at his necktie as if pulling an extended finger, Dangerfield vents his disdain for his nagging, social-climbing wife (Adrienne Barbeau) and her high-class friends by clearing a fancy restaurant with a fusillade of flagrant, but hardly fragrant, farting. *Back to School* grossed out some of its audience, but it also grossed over a $100 million.

By the late 1980s farts were bursting across the comedy screen like Chinese firecrackers, not only in Hollywood's B world (where a steeplechase horse farts into Robert Stack's face in *Caddyshack II*, an ugly junkyard mutt breaks wind at Tom Hanks in *Turner and Hooch*, and extraterrestrials fume in the outer space vacuum of Mel Brooks's *Spaceballs*) but also in middle-brow fare such as Neil Simon's *Biloxi Blues*, where a flatulent bunkmate provokes Matthew Broderick into wearing a gas mask, and even in the Oscar-winning film *Rain Man*, which sneaks in a stealthy-but-deadly; while Tom Cruise and Dustin Hoffman are squeezed together in a phone booth, Cruise asks, "Did you fart?" Hoffman, playing Cruise's autistic brother, remains as silent as his flatus.

The fart was certainly wafting in polite company by 1994, when Walt Disney Studios, once a bastion of middle-American propriety and tight-assed taste, became woozy from the box-office aroma of flatulence. (According to several animators who worked for him, Uncle Walt was himself notoriously and blissfully flatulent in the presence of others.) Disney's animated blockbuster, *The Lion King*, not only features a warthog named Punbaa whose farting power is prodigious, but includes a song about it called "Hakuna Matata" (Swahili for "no worries"), which was nominated for an Academy Award. According to the song, "When he was a young warthog he found his aroma lacked a certain appeal, he could clear the savannah after every meal." Ernie Sabella, the voice of Punbaa, told *The New York Times* that farting was not originally in the script but added on the spot when Nathan Lane (voicing Punbaa's meerkat sidekick Timon) encouraged him to make an impromptu fart noise while they were recording the script. The directors laughed and decided it would be a great idea. "We never thought we would use it," said Sabella, but Punbaa's farts became a running gag.

Disney's 1997 live-action cartoon *George of the Jungle* (a remake of a late 1960s TV cartoon parody of Tarzan) continued the new tradition by featuring an intellectual gorilla with a recurrent intestinal problem. In another Disney film that same year,

Rocket Man, astronaut Harland Williams's diet of NASA "space beans" creates a serious gas crisis in his space suit. Tethered to another earthling on the surface of Mars, he watches his fart move as a large bubble through their joint air-supply tube like a rat through a boa constrictor. "It wasn't me," he tells his companion, even though there's nobody else around for 125 million miles. Disney rounded off 1997 with another recycle job called *Flubber*, highlighted by what one newspaper called "hi-tech flatulence"— the gooey little title character, a kind of shiny green Pillsbury Doughboy, working its way through the villain's body and then being blasted out of his ass with a fart.

Only one actor, Harland Williams, publicly complained about the direction that his career and Hollywood were going. He told the *Los Angeles Times*, "I've been in three movies [*Rocket Man*, *Down Periscope*, and *Dumb and Dumber*] and all of them had flatulence jokes. I gotta get a script that had Pepto-Bismol soaked in it or something. Don't get me wrong—everyone loves a great flatulence joke. But I'm interested in cerebral stuff as opposed to intestinal."

Williams was onto something. The movie fart had become so gratuitous that it was losing its impact. His previous film, *Down Periscope* (1996), explores the dangers of gassy food in a submarine during not-so-silent running. In 1995's *Grumpier Old Men*, two flatulent old farts (Jack Lemmon and Walter Matthau) find themselves upstaged by Matthau's one-eyed flatulent dog. In *The Road to Wellville*, a 1994 biopic of John H. Kellogg—the health guru, breakfast cereal magnate, and self-professed "enemy of the civilized colon"—farts are little more than devices to pep up the dialogue. Geraldine Chaplin plays a crazy aunt whose recurrent farting spells provide *Home for the Holidays* (1995) with intermittent humor. In *Dennis the Menace* (1996), Christopher Lloyd eats his way through a bowl of beans in order to find a handcuff key at the bottom, only to fart so hard into a fireplace that the flames nearly engulf him. In *Jack* (1996), the story of a ten-year-old boy trapped in a forty-year-old body, Robin Williams joins his fifth-grade classmates in a farting contest. In *3 Ninjas Kick Back* (1995), a little league baseball catcher, played by twelve-year-old Brian

Wagner, passes gas horrendous enough to knock out infielders as he runs the bases. *Spawn*, a 1997 live-action remake of a comic book series, has a ghoulishly greasepainted clown from hell (John Leguizamo) who blows green gas out of his ass and jokes that he gets a pair of wings every time a demon farts. Even a popular art-house Mexican import, *Like Water for Chocolate* (1993), based on Laura Esquivel's novel, has a female character who takes vengeance on her older sister by fixing a meal packed with enough flatulent factors to nearly blow out her asshole. Among prize-winning computer animation films was a 1992 short called *Gas Planet*, in which aliens consume pods that make them fart uncontrollably. And thanks to a new crop of charmless comics (think Pauly Shore) starring in low-budget flicks aimed primarily at the video market, meaningless farts for farts' sake became the cinematic equivalents of feeble freeps, worth two points at best.

By the time Eddie Murphy staged a comeback in 1996 with *The Nutty Professor* after a string of box-office disappointments, he knew that farts were golden—the more the merrier. One of several characters he plays in the film uses an entire volley of farts at the dinner table to voice his appreciation for a sumptuous meal and to reinforce his dominance over his family. When asked later by the press if he was perhaps overdoing it, Murphy admitted that his film did have "more than our flatulence quota." But Disney Studios executive Jeffrey Katzenberg disagreed; when asked the same question, he defended the fart frequency in *The Nutty Professor*, proclaiming, "Every movie should have exactly that number."

But by now, only occasionally was a fart being used creatively. For example, in *Liar Liar* (1997), the story of a slick lawyer rendered incapable of telling a lie, Jim Carrey turns a popular farting scenario on its head when he steps out of an elevator filled with business people gasping and waving their hands in front of their faces. Turning around on his heel, he proudly exclaims, "It was *me*!" (Two years earlier, in *Dumb and Dumber*, Carrey also did a hilarious take on lighting farts when he tried to amuse a stodgy bunch of preppies at a ski resort by lying on the floor, rolling his ass up over his head, and flicking his Bic.)

The power of fart humor itself was highlighted in the late

1997 film *Good Will Hunting*. An uncommunicative young man (Matt Damon) sits passively through countless sessions with his therapist (Robin Williams yet again), until finally one day Robins stumbles upon a breakthrough. He confesses to his patient that his own ex-wife farted in her sleep, louder and louder, until one night she woke herself up and asked, "Was that the dog?" The scene provokes laughter not only with the audience but, in a therapeutic way, with the young man as well.

So far, no movie has been made about the fart itself, though *Gas Planet* comes close. But there was a near miss when radio personality Howard Stern had a film in development called *The Adventures of Fartman* (see Stern's own story in chapter 11). Though the film never made it through the pipeline, Stern did showcase his Fartman character in his 1997 biopic *Private Parts*.

Howard Stern also added yet another dimension, literally, to farting in a 1995 mail-order video called *Butt Bongo Fiesta*. During a jungle skit, Stern is a Tarzan-like character rescuing a maiden in distress (Jessica Hahn) from a mad elephant. Unschooled in etiquette, Stern's Jungle Man celebrates his victory by farting in Miss Hahn's face. Thanks to video technology, the fart registers as a billowing green cloud, and viewers wearing the 3-D glasses sold with *Butt Bongo Fiesta* are treated to the full depth of Jungle Man's diet of fruits and nuts. At this point, until the hologram is perfected, there seems to be nowhere else the cinematic fart can go.

The popularity of flatulence at the local cineplex assured that it would soon be coming to a screen even nearer to you, i.e., your TV set. But movies are one thing and network TV is quite another, and so the fart, up until recently at least, had to be handled gingerly.

An early fart was sneaked into prime-time TV in 1969 on NBC's *The Smothers Brothers Comedy Hour* when Pat Paulsen, a regular on the show, portrayed a dealer of cheap magic tricks and comedy gags in a skit written by unknown writers Rob Reiner and Steve Martin. When Paulsen sat down in a chair to demonstrate a whoopee cushion, the audience heard a quick fart sound; the punch line came when he stood up and discovered that there was no whoopee cushion in the chair. But since NBC's censors were more frightened of the show's radical political humor, they let it pass.

It was left to British television to bring what was perhaps the first running fart gag into people's living rooms. In a 1976–80 BBC comedy called *The Fall and Rise of Reginald Perrin*, a boss (played by Leonard Rossiter) humiliated his underlings weekly with a special Japanese whoopee cushion chair in his office. Every time someone sat down or stood up, the chair emitted a flatulent honk. Another seventies BBC comedy, *Are You Being Served?*, offered a couple of characters with gas problems. And on the BBC's hilarious but too brief *Fawlty Towers*, John Cleese's 1979-81 sitcom about the mismanagement of a small hotel, several episodes showed that someone had tampered with the Fawlty Towers sign out front and changed it into Farty Towels. (The latter two series were later picked up for American broadcast by PBS.)

In the United States about that same time, Johnny Carson broke the TV fart barrier during a popular annual segment of his *Tonight Show* that honored award-winning TV commercials from around the world. A Japanese commercial showed several cute children playing in a hot tub. Suddenly, to the embarrassment of one little boy, the bubbles from his fart broke the surface of the water. Since the fart was foreign, the farter was nearly an infant, and the hour was late (after 11:30 P.M.), NBC's standards and practices watchdogs literally let it fly through the air.

Still, farting was a no-no on American TV, and it would take a few more years before Johnny Carson, speaking through his ongoing Carnac the Magnificent character, admonished the audience with "May the bird of flatulence squat on your face." When ABC ran *Blazing Saddles* as a movie of the week, its editors erased the cowboys' roundelay of farting and overdubbed the sounds of whinnying horses—and that silent-but-deadly TV version is the one that ABC and the Comedy Central cable network play to this day.

The word *fart* finally emanated from the vast wasteland on the evening of April 2, 1982—thanks to radio. The program was *NBC Magazine*, an unsuccessful attempt by the peacock network to come up with its own version of CBS's *60 Minutes*. On that momentous Friday night, Douglas Kiker hosted a segment titled "X-Rated Radio" that blew the whistle on the new "shock jock" phenomenon. "What you are about to hear is going to shock and disgust you, because it's vulgar, even obscene," Kiker intoned. "It's X-rated radio, barnyard radio. . . ." Cut to Howard Stern sitting at the microphone at Washington, D.C., station WWDC, blaring, "Hey, man, I hears your pappy is so disgusting that he takes a bubble bath by farting in a mud puddle." There it was, in front of America: *fart!* Kiker leapt back onscreen to demand rhetorically, "Can't something be done to get this filth off the air?" Apparently not, but *NBC Magazine* itself got the boot three months later.

With the coming of breakthrough programming like CBS's *All in the Family* (1971-83), the crepitus occasionally crept into humorous situations, especially if the show aired after the eight o'clock family hour that was instituted for several years in the mid-seventies. In an episode late in the decade, an outraged Archie Bunker (Carroll O'Connor) complained to his wife Edith (Jean Stapleton) that he had been trapped in an elevator with a man who not only farted but smiled about it.

NBC's late-night *Saturday Night Live* dabbled in light verbal fart humor, but never faced it full on. In the 1981-82 season, a family of mutants living next to a nuclear plant developed a new orifice called the "blowhole." Another episode was based on euphemisms. "Shall I cut the cheese?" said one cast member, dangling a knife over a block of Cheddar. There was also a mock commercial for Colon Blow high-fiber cereal. But the closest that this iconoclastic show came to the ass itself was showing Dan Aykroyd's butt crack sneaking above his belt while he bent down to repair a refrigerator.

The first network TV show to unapologetically embrace the fart as a laugh-getter was Fox's *In Living Color*, which debuted in 1990 as an antidote to the limp yuppie humor that had taken over *Saturday Night Live*. An early episode of *In Living Color* features a mock commercial for a new product, called Flatuscents, that transforms internal gas into fine fragrances. One scent is "New Car." Tommy Davidson and Jim Carrey are driving along when it becomes obvious from Carrey's blissed-out smile that he has slipped off a quiet fart. A moment later Davidson sniffs the air and asks, "Hey, is this a new car?" "No," Carrey replies. "I just had a chili dog at the ball game."

On another episode, Carrey's most demented character, Fire Marshall Bill, gives himself a nitroglycerine enema, offers his finger to Anne-Marie Johnson to be pulled, and announces, "Get ready for a scene from *Backdraft*." Carrey, as it turned out, was merely warming up; he would soon cross over into films to become Hollywood's foremost *fartiste*.

Among *In Living Color*'s running characters, still popular in reruns, is a street bum named Anton Jackson, played by Damon Wayans. From episode to episode, despite his ragged appearance and noxious body odor, Anton somehow finds himself mixing in polite company—in a restaurant, in court, in a suburban home—where he invariably slides out a silent-but-deadly that flabbergasses the entire cast. He always nonchalantly waves it off as he mumbles lukewarm apologies.

Other prime-time TV shows followed. ABC's *Roseanne* had already touched upon farting in the first episode of the 1989 fall season, when Roseanne's older daughter, Becky, suffered public humiliation by letting off a loud one while she was giving a speech at school. Now sitcoms could explore the subject more earnestly. For example, in a 1997 episode of NBC's popular *3rd Rock from the Sun*, farting was used as a metaphor to demonstrate marital bliss when Jane Curtin's character let a fart to establish pointedly that she shared a considerable comfort zone with her husband (John Lithgow). Then, as they hug in a final embrace, one of them cuts a second fart. "Was that you or me?" Lithgow asks Curtin in a display of true simpatico. They were one, and so were their farts.

But these were relatively tasteful explorations of the social embarrassment and taboos of farting. The subject wasn't used for purely gratuitous effect on a major network sitcom until a February 1997 episode of ABC's *Drew Carey Show*, in which one of Carey's friends pulls a prank on him by dubbing farts onto an industrial video he's made for his bosses. Every time Carey bends over or lifts a leg in the video, he emits a loud or squeaking fart. (This episode was apparently inspired by an underground video called *Pastor Gas*, in which actual footage of quirky Texas televangelist Robert Tilton's litany of facial grimaces was overdubbed by farts.)

Even demure Brooke Shields's NBC sitcom *Suddenly Susan* was not immune to such gratuitous fart humor. In a fall 1997 episode, a dog farts at a funeral. Speaking of flatulent animals, *Seinfeld*, in a 1996 episode called "The Rye," explores the potency of horsepower when Cosmo Kramer (Michael Richards) temporarily takes over a friend's Central Park carriage route and feeds the horse a large, economy can of Beefarino that makes the poor nag's farts smell so badly that neither Kramer nor his customers riding in back can handle the odor.

When the *Tonight Show with Jay Leno* replaced Johnny Carson in 1994, farts became almost a common topic of conversation. Leslie Nielsen, in a whimsical mood, made various fart noises one night, and comedians Martin Mull and Kelsey Grammer, on separate occasions, discussed the French *farteur* Le Petomane. Whoopi Goldberg told Leno how her propensity for farting inspired her friends to call her a human whoopee cushion—Whoopi for short. Bette Midler told Leno a joke about a lady who couldn't hear her own farts. Scottish comic Billy Connolly described to Leno his cultural displacement upon first arriving in America: "I felt like a fart in a space suit." Garry Shandling commented during an appearance that you never know if your love relationship is going well until one of you lets loose with the first fart. Howard Stern spoke at length with Leno about his *Adventures of Fartman* project, and other guests, including critic Gene Siskel, mentioned Stern's aborted film while sitting in Leno's hot seat.

But flatulence's greatest moment on late-night TV occurred on July 2, 1998, when Howard Stern (once again) appeared on "Magic" Johnson's Fox-based *The Magic Hour* with three people in tow who could fart on cue. This wasn't just folks sitting around discussing farts. This time the cheese cutting was real . . . and live on stage.

Farting even wafted into TV drama, beginning in 1991, when a featured character, Douglas Brackman Jr. (Alan Rachins), in NBC's *L.A. Law* develops farting problems whenever he finds himself in an intimate moment with a woman. In a 1993 episode of NBC's award-winning *Law & Order* called "Scoundrels," two detectives (Chris Noth and Jerry Orbach) question a woman whose knickknack invention business includes a board set called

Flatulence: The Game. (When the cops follow their noses, she turns out to be in cahoots with the villain.) And in an early episode of NBC's smash hit *ER*, in the fall of 1994, a patient being examined by several emergency room staffers suddenly gasses them with a whoosh of farting.

In 1993, breaking wind was played for deadpan laughs on an Emmy-winning, made-for-HBO drama called *Barbarians at the Gate*, (from Bryan Burrough and John Helyar's bestseller). RJR CEO Ray Johnson (played by James Garner) oversaw the development in 1989 of a smokeless cigarette called Premier. Costing $350 million to develop and another $150 million to promote—a cool half-billion dollars in all—Premier turned out to be the Edsel of cigarettes. The major problem, as detailed in the movie, was that test groups complained that Premiers "taste like shit and smell like farts." Upon hearing this news, Johnson bitterly wonders if that should be the cigarette brand's slogan: "Tastes like shit and smells like farts!" That appraisal led to a pack of one-liners throughout the rest of the film.

For a while, a sanitizing wall quarantined TV commercials from the fart-saturated entertainment around them. But that changed in 1995, when a mustard commercial showcased a gentleman in the back of a limousine squirting Grey Poupon onto his hot dog from a plastic bottle. The suspiciously crepitating sound created by air (mustard gas?) in the bottle causes the chauffeur to raise a reproving eyebrow, prompting the gentleman in the back seat to utter, "Pardon me." This ad led, two years later, to a Toyota Corolla spot in which an older couple argue whether to put their power windows up or down. Suddenly their grandchild in the back seat lets a fart and presumably shits in its diapers. The grandparents look at each other and exclaim, "Down!"

As adult-oriented TV animation proliferated in the 1990s, it was the perfect format for flatulent humor—first on cable, later on the Fox network. The fart furnished entire plots for two segments of Nickelodeon's *The Ren & Stimpy Show*, an imaginative cartoon series starring Ren, a rheumy-eyed Mexican Chihuahua, and Stimpy, a fat, neurotic cat. In 1992's "Son of Stimpy" (also known as "Stimpy's First Trouser Cough" and available on videotape as

Have Yourself a Stinky Little Christmas), Stimpy returns to a Christmas past to search for Stinky, the first little bundle of gas he ever passed. He says he'd been watching TV when "Something came out of my butt." Though Ren refuses to believe that Stinky exists, Stimpy spends the next few years trying to reunite with his long-lost friend. Finally, Stimpy discovers that the orphaned Stinky has also been looking for him because it wants "back in." In another episode called "Bride of Stimpy," the cat goes looking for yet another lost fart.

Almost from the moment that *The Simpsons* first aired on Fox in 1989, young Bart Simpson, the wayward son, grossed out his parents with body-humor sass, such as "Eat my shorts." In one episode he sings "Beans, beans, the musical fruit" to his class at school. And among his many punishments is writing "I will not make flatulent noises in class" a hundred times on the blackboard.

On MTV's *Beavis and Butt-head*, which premiered in 1993, farts were only a small part of the body humor that underpinned the show's hilarity—but an important part nonetheless. *Los Angeles Times* TV critic Howard Rosenberg observed, "Beavis and Butt-head have huh-huh-huhed their way to MTV fame as wise-cracking connoisseurs of bad music videos and virtuosos of coarse mischief and flatulence." Beavis in particular is prone to "burning burritos," and Butt-head often calls him a "fartknocker." A common exchange between the scraggly adolescents is "Pull my finger." Critics complained, but as the show's creator, Mike Judge, put it, "These characters are like guys I knew in junior high. Vulgar schoolyard humor is just the way they are." They became so popular that in 1997 NBC launched a new program called *Men Behaving Badly* that starred real-life human versions of Beavis and Butt-head, acting stupid and letting farts.

But the last word came from Comedy Central's 1997 entry into the farting sweepstakes, *South Park*, a demented cartoon about four third-graders in the snowy Colorado Rockies. One of the kids develops a case of flame-shooting farts after space aliens probe his asshole in the very first episode, called "Cartman Gets an Anal Probe." In a later episode the town's parents protest the airing of a popular TV show about two numskull characters named

Terence and Phillip who do nothing for half an hour but insult and break wind at each other in an excoriating spoof not only of Beavis and Butt-head but also the growing trend of farts for farts' sake. Where else is there to go from there?

Perhaps Terence and Phillip will soon get their own TV show—for real—and when it becomes a hit, Hollywood will do the $50 million movie version with high-tech special-effects, including hologram farts and Smell-O-Vision.

JUMPIN JACK FLASH, SHE'S GOT GAS, GAS, GAS

During her visits on late-night talk shows, comedienne Caryn Johnson admitted that she picked up the first half of her stage name, Whoopi Goldberg, because she frequently passed gas and sounded like a walking whoopee cushion. "I had ulcers," she confessed, "and my doctor said, 'If you need to let them go, then let them go'!" In an early one-woman show called *The Telephone*, one of Whoopi's routines was "The Dance of the Seven Flatulences." And when this star of the film *Jumpin' Jack Flash* hosted the Academy Awards in March 1996, Bette Midler's "Wind Beneath My Wings" won an Oscar for Best Song, prompting Whoopi to remark to the world-at-large that she had her own wind but it wasn't beneath her wings.

In her 1997 autobiography, *Book*, Whoopi dedicated an entire chapter ("Wind") to farting. Among her observations were, "There should be some scanning device built into all new elevators that lets people know if there's a fart on board. . . . Maybe there could be a big sign (FART ENCLOSED) to warn people away . . . because being trapped in an elevator with someone else's fart is one of the worst fates known to modern man." She admitted that she calls her own farts "tree monkeys" because "tree monkeys make the same farty sound as I do. It's a funny little sound. It would almost be cute, if it wasn't followed by the smell," and she shared her mother's down-home wisdom through the expression "More room out than in," meaning "there's more room outside your body for this little air bubble than there is inside." Best of all, she retold the flatulent origin of her name Whoopi. "The name lingers," she said, "like a good fart."

"I think flatulence is one of the greatest joys of life!" she told CBS's late-night host Tom Snyder while promoting *Book*. He responded, "People who speak rectally speak to me." Then the normally tight-assed host told a fart joke about Queen Elizabeth.

11

THE ADVENTURES OF FARTMAN

He wrote a movie, Fartman, *on which all his hopes were pinned—*
A superhero powered by the force of his own wind;
The flick was never made—some say the plot was too high-class,
Or else the deal fell through because the script ran out of gas."

—Mad *magazine, 1995*

The dark, antifart forces are out there, intimidating each and every one of us who treasures a good butt blast. In such a thick atmosphere of oppression, is there a savior, some superhero who can blow away America's fear of flatulence?

Yes, it's Fartman!—faster than air from a whoopee cushion, more powerful than a pound of Ex-Lax, able to leap tall enema carts in a single bound, and who, disguised as Howard Stern, mild-mannered nationally syndicated radio personality for a metropolitan station, fights for liberty, truth, justice, and the American way!

Stern broadcasts every weekday morning from the Manhattan radio studios of WXRK to over five million people across North America. He loves to let farts into the microphone and record them so that his sidekick and sound effects man, Fred Norris, can put them into a computer and play them back at appropriate (and inappropriate) times during the program. In 1995 Stern even farted directly ("cheek to cheek") into the face of his producer, Gary Dell'Abate, after winning a football bet. "Farting," Stern told one TV interviewer, "is one of the most wonderful things—it's like a symphony to me!"

He broached the subject on the airwaves as early as 1978, while broadcasting from rock station KRNW in Westchester County, New York. A fellow disc jockey, Bruce Figler, recalled the time when Stern played a Neil Young song, "Four Strong Winds," then explained to his listeners why he thought it was about flatulence. "Here it was between six and seven in the morning, and Howard's doing fart routines on the air," said Figler.

When not farting or playing back his old, sampled farts, Stern sometimes inquires about or comments on his guests' farts. For example, in 1996, while interviewing Sandy Allen, who at seven-foot-seven is the world's tallest woman, he remarked, "Your farts must register on the Richter scale, right?"

He also sent his roving interviewer, Stuttering John Melendez, to ask baseball legend Ted Williams, "Did you ever accidentally fart in the catcher's face?" Williams, not amused by the question, demanded, "Who the hell are you?" and cut the interview short, muttering, "What kind of shit . . . ?" When Melendez later asked Reggie Jackson the same question, the former Yankee and Oakland A's slugger replied, "Yes, and if you hang out long enough, I'll fart in *your* face."

In his best-selling 1993 autobiography *Private Parts*, Howard Stern traced his fascination with flatulence back to his childhood, when his parents took him into Manhattan for supper and an evening at Radio City Music Hall. When the unfamiliar food and his nervous eating habits prompted little Howard to complain about gas pangs at the show, his father advised him, "At the intermission, after the Rockettes are finished, go out in the lobby, walk over to the side, and let a few out." But the kid was so intimidated by the huge art deco lobby that he couldn't bring himself to break wind there, even when his father prodded him: "Go ahead, do it. Do it already. What's the problem with you, you're ruining the day." The night ended with his dad stopping on the way home, dragging Howard into the bathroom of a hotel, and ordering him to fart. "Now I'm sitting in this filthy stall in this seedy hotel with my old man pacing outside the stall," Stern wrote, "waiting to hear me pass gas. He's pacing, and my mother and sister are outside, alone in the car." The pressure on his bowels increased, but anxiety tightened his sphincter to the point where nothing could get out.

This early trauma would later fan the flames for Howard Stern's most glorious on-air character, Fartman, a superhuman crepitator who really flies by the seat of his pants. Created by a comic named Rodger Bumpass (his real name), Fartman originally appeared on a 1980 National Lampoon LP called *The White Album*, which Stern himself credits for his inspiration. In a one-minute skit, complete with plenty of rip-roaring sound effects, Bumpass delivers his spiel in an echoed, stentorian voice suitable for a man of steel bowels: "I'm Fartman. My farts have amazing powers. I can fart so hard that I can fly through the air. I can gas evildoers and knock them unconscious. Or I can light my farts and turn them into a devastating wall of flame, ah-*hah*!" But then, as we hear the intruding noises of an office, Fartman changes his tune. "I'd be a great superhero if I did these things, but I don't. I work in an office and I don't let anybody know about my powers." The skit fades as female voices in the background disdainfully groan about his farting.

After Howard Stern became one of the early terrors of shock radio, he decided to put himself in charge of U.S. foreign policy. He routinely called embassies whenever there was some new crisis in the world, yelling his demands at whoever he could get on the phone. While broadcasting in Washington, D.C., he complained officially about the lousy treatment Lech Walesa's Solidarity Party members were getting from the Polish government during the latest military crackdown. As Stern later recounted, "I got on the air, called the Polish embassy, and actually got through to the Polish ambassador, farted into the phone, and the rest is history."

"I fart so hard I fly through the air," he boasted, parroting Roger Bumpass's earlier Fartman. "I can light my farts and create a devastating wall of flame."

Like any superhero, Stern's Fartman had his own credo: "My tushy rules and drools. My digestive system pumps foul air for truth and justice." In subsequent years the U.S.-based representatives of the Ayatollah (Iran), General Noriega (Panama), Qaddafi (Libya), and Saddam Hussein (Iraq), to name a few, earned the ass-wrenching wrath of Fartman. When army troops shot down hundreds of student demonstrators in Beijing's Tiananmen Square in 1989, Fartman warned the Chinese consulate that, at his instigation, the F.A.O. Schwarz department store would stop selling Chinese checkers.

The arrival of Fartman was always accompanied by a flourish of Wagnerian music. "I'm Fartman," he'd announce in an echo-chambered baritone. "My odorous back end whistles stinky wind in the face of adversity. I have the super sphincter that saved the planet. My brownish wind will hit my enemies in the face like doody [shit] pie. And though I am a grown man and protect the world from all that is wrong, I speak like a friggin' infant with words like stinky and doody!"

Fartman went nationwide when Stern, catching a good tail-wind, flew to Los Angeles to present an award for the best heavy metal/hard rock video at the MTV Video Music Awards in 1992. "It was," Stern would say five years later, "one of the defining moments of my career." The event was a stuffy affair that revealed the hollowness of modern rock's rebellion. Stern discovered just how square and phony his rock 'n' roll compatriots were when he decided to fly onto the stage dressed as Fartman. The only celebrity who agreed to be his co-presenter was actor Luke Perry, a regular on Fox TV's *Beverly Hills 90210*. When the time came for Fartman's entrance, Stern descended from thirty feet above the stage in a cheesy green and yellow costume, his pitted ass cheeks protruding from the back of his shorts, as Perry announced to the crowd over the amplified sounds of farting: "From a land far away and long, long ago, it's a bird, it's a plane, it's a really bad smell. Ladies and gentleman, F-F-F-F-Fartman!"

Stern landed and mooned the audience. Then, as the crowd went into a frenzy, he aimed his flabby posterior at the podium and declared "the greatest power of all!" A boom rocked the hall as the podium exploded in a billow of smoke and light. "Yes, you may be laughing at my ass now," Stern said, "but when my movie *Fartman* becomes number one, all of Hollywood will kiss my ass!" Sadly, the one line he didn't utter was, "I just flew in from the East Coast, and boy is my ass tired." Supermannequin Cindy Crawford, unimpressed with Stern, remarked after the show, "I thought it was disgusting, and if my ass looked like that, I wouldn't show it on national television."

In late June 1992 Stern returned to the West Coast to meet with Mike DeLuca, president of production at New Line Cinema, a company best known for its *Nightmare on Elm Street* films. A preliminary contract was signed to get an upcoming *Fartman* into the development pipeline. During this Los Angeles sojourn Stern also made his first appearance on the *Tonight Show with Jay Leno*. Among many outrageous comments, Stern revealed to Jay and to millions of late-night middle-American viewers that he would soon be turning his "pet" project into a butt-*bang*-o! fiesta film called *The Adventures of Fartman*. The ratings for Jay Leno's June 24 show with Howard Stern were his highest since he'd taken over Johnny Carson's desk earlier in the year.

As it turned out, Fartman's superhuman exhaust could not blow down the barriers of Hollywood's film industry. New Line Cinema, having second thoughts, told Stern that his Fartman would have to be PG rated. Stern wanted something more on the level of an R; how do you make a wholesome PG movie about a guy who blows shit gas out of his bunghole? Also, New Line's bean counters demanded control over all merchandising connected to Fartman, an arrangement that Stern found unacceptable. Furthermore, Hollywood blockbuster producer Ivan Reitman, who would later produce Stern's 1997 film version of *Private Parts*, advised him that *The Adventures of Fartman* would likely ruin his chance of breaking into mainstream films later on. Ultimately Stern's reply to New Line Cinema was "Blow it out your ass," or words to that effect.

Fartman made the news again, however. One of Stern's regular contributors, Chris Giglio, who bills himself as the King of All Messengers, frequently calls TV and radio phone-in programs to drop Howard Stern's name on the unsuspecting hosts, and then phones Stern's radio show to play back the tape. Immediately after New York's World Trade Center was bombed on February 26, 1993, Giglio made a phony phone call to CNN during the news network's live disaster coverage, claiming that he was trapped on the eightieth floor. The screener duly put him on the air—internationally! Asked by CNN anchor Bernard Shaw what he thought might have caused the fatal blast that killed six people and injured over a thousand, Giglio blamed it on a gas leak from Fartman.

Fartman did make it to celluloid, finally, when the opening scene of Stern's Hollywood debut, *Private Parts*, reprised the superhero's disastrous appearance, pitted bare ass and all, at the MTV awards show. And on the Arts & Entertainment cable network, the series *Biography* regularly replays its own hour-long tribute to Howard Stern, complete with Fartman's real-life podium-blistering performance. Perhaps we have not seen the last of this caped crepitator after all.

DOCTOR, MY FARTS!

Going to doctors, taking off our clothes, and putting ourselves at their mercy is one of life's most humbling duties, so naturally there are lots of doctor jokes, including a few in the fart department. Here's a common one: A lady goes to her doctor and complains, "I'm worried. My farts don't smell." He tells her to get undressed and lie down on her stomach on the examination table. While he's peering into her rectum with a tiny flashlight, she cuts loose with a fart. The doctor straightens up and walks over to where he keeps his instruments.

"Doctor," she asks, "are you going to operate on my ass?"

"No," he replies, "I'm going to operate on your nose."

There's a slight variation on this joke that Bette Midler told on the *Tonight Show with Jay Leno* in 1994. The lady complains to the doctor of her "silent gas emissions." After experiencing one of the woman's farts during his examination, the doctor tells her he needs to "check your hearing."

In yet another variation, told by Jackie "The Joke Man" Martling, a guy tells his doctor, "My hearing's going bad. I can't even hear myself fart." The doctor gives him some pills. The guy asks, "Will they make me hear better?"

"No," says the doctor. "They'll make you fart louder."

Then there's the guy who goes to his proctologist and says, "Doc, I just can't stop farting." The doctor walks across the room and picks up an eight-foot pole with a hook at the end of it. The patient blanches, his eyes bug out. "Doc, what's that for?"

"To open the goddamn window. I'm suffocating in here!"

This one's been popular for many years: An Indian chief's squaw goes to the reservation doctor and says, "Big chief no fart."

The doctor gives her some pills and tells her, "Have him take three of these a day."

A week later the squaw returns and tells the doctor, "Big chief no fart."

He gives her another vial and says, "Have him take five of these a day."

Next week she returns. "Big chief no fart."

This time the doctor fills up a vial with ten pills and tells her, "Have him take them all."

Next day the squaw arrives back at the doctor's office looking glum. "What's wrong," he asks.

"Big fart, no chief!"

Here's one of my favorites. "I want you to eat two bowls of chili beans every day," the doctor tells his pregnant young patient.

"Why?" she asks.

"Well, you're farting for two now."

Finally, here's one for pun lovers. A Tokyo-based Toyota executive goes to a proctologist. He says he's a nervous wreck because every time he lets a fart, it comes out sounding like "Honda," and within the competitive corporate offices of Toyota that's nothing short of blasphemy. After the examination, the doctor tells him, "Ah so, Mr. Yagashima, you have abscess between butt cheeks."

"Yes, and?"

"Well, Mr. Yagashima, abscess makes the fart go 'Honda'!"

12

FUN WITH FARTS

What are men anyway but balloons on legs,
a lot of blown-up bladders? . . .
[A] man's a bubble, all air, nothing else.

—*Gaius Petronius,* Satyricon *(first century)*

Boys will be boys, and one thing that most boys love to do is fart
and laugh about it. If we can't fart, we'll make flatulent noises
with our mouths, our sweaty palms, our armpits, or with any number of toys and gimmicks available to us at novelty shops. Even
when we grow up we don't necessarily outgrow these things.
Farting is a guy thing. Women just don't understand the gales of
masculine belly laughter that erupt at the tail end of someone's fart.

I guess part of the reason is that women are brought up to be
more mature and genteel than men are. But nature also wires
women differently, particularly when it comes to smelling odors.
Richard L. Doty, director of the Smell and Taste Center at the
University of Pennsylvania, published the results of a landmark
1984 study that graded the olfactory sensibilities of 1,900 men and
women through the use of a "micro-encapsulated odor test"—a
fancy term for scratch 'n' sniff. Doty found that women of all ages
could identify odors more accurately than their male counterparts.
"Women have a better sense of smell, period," he said. More
recently, in 1997, researchers at the University of Minnesota

Medical School reported that men and women appear to use different parts of the brain during smell-related tasks. It's probably safe
to say that women are not likely any time soon to amuse themselves at soirees by lighting each other's blue darters or initiating
conversations with the words "Pull my finger." These are joys that
men must be content to keep among themselves.

According to Eddie Brandt, who worked as an arranger for
the Spike Jones Orchestra in the 1940s, a fart was called a "Toby"
among the band members and was punishable by two slugs on the
arm. The origin of these poot punches can be found in the ancient
boys' game of "touch wood," in which anyone who farts on a play-
ground suddenly becomes "it" and has to run to a designated tree
or wooden box and touch it before his classmates pound on him.
(In a variant of this game, when somebody farts, everybody has to
run and touch wood, and the last kid who does takes a thumping.)
This game is also known as "touch bone and whistle": If you fart,
your companions chase you down, pinch you hard "to the bone,"
and whistle. (These amusements may have their origins in primitive
religions—see chapter 8—that demanded tributes be paid to the
deities in charge of the stomach, bowels, and rectum. Perhaps the
supplicant had to touch the altar as he deposited a fart or a bowel
movement as thanks for his good digestion.)

Then there are farting contests and fart-lighting demonstra-
tions, reportedly held at schools and universities for centuries. A
couple of scholars vaguely recall a fart-lighting episode in *Tom
Brown's School Days*, Thomas Hughes's influential 1857 novel
about British public schools, but a check of various editions failed
to turn anything up. Perhaps the book was bowdlerized and the
expurgated portion has not been reinstated to its proper place in
present-day editions.

In his memoirs about his World War II days in uniform,
British comedian Spike Milligan of *Goon Show* fame recalled how
his fellow soldiers performed with gastrointestinal fortitude:

> It was after lights out that some of the most hysterical
> moments occurred. Those who had been drinking heavily
> soon made it known by great asphyxiating farts that rendered

their owners unconscious and cleared the beds all round. There were even more gentlemen who performed feats with their unwanted nether winds that not even great Petomane could have eclipsed; simply, they set fire to them. The "artiste" would bend down, his assistant stood by with a lighted match. When the "artiste" let off, he ignited it. Using this method I have seen sheets of blue flames up to a foot in length. Old timers, by conserving their fuel, could scorch a Tudor Rose on the wall. There was Signaler "X" whose control of the anal sphincter allowed him to pass morse code messages. With my own ears I heard him send S.O.S. On these occasions I, like others, lay in bed crying with laughter.

In another book, *Silly Verse for Kids*, Milligan rhapsodized: "Maverick Prowels had rumbling bowels that thundered in the night, And every time he farted, the sheets turned up in fright!"

In *Semi-Tough*, a 1972 best-selling novel about professional football, Dan Jenkins introduced T.J. Lambert, perhaps the literary world's biggest gasbag and guy's guy since Zola's Jésus-Christ. In an early scene, Lambert,

our big old defensive end from Tennessee, hiked his leg and made a noise like a watermelon being dropped on concrete out of a four-story building.

He sure can fart is what I'm getting at. And he can do it as many different times as you can imagine. And almost any time he wants to. . . . As a matter of fact, T. J. has always claimed that he can fart in a lot of different colors, too, but of course I don't know anyone who ever cared enough to check up on it.

In the course of the novel, T. J.'s farts allow him to distract kickers and chase off opposing players scrambling for a fumbled ball. But Jenkins's best story concerns T. J.'s honeymoon night in a Tennessee motel with his bride, Donna Lou, when the big guy decides to pull a prank on her:

"I was gonna give her my Class A Boomer," T. J. says. "When she come out of the bathroom, I was gonna cut one that would jar the window shades, and then for the rest of our married life there wouldn't be no trouble about me fartin' around the house. You never know whether a woman likes that kind of thing."

What happened of course was that Donna Lou came out of the bathroom and for the only time in his life, old T. J.'s talent betrayed him. Instead of farting, he shit all over the bed.

When Donna Lou gets drunk enough these days, she enjoys telling the story herself and she refers to T. J. as "old Rudolph Valentino over there." At which point T. J. is liable to unleash his Class A Boomer.

In a dream sequence in the 1995 film *Dumb and Dumber*, Jim Carrey's oblivious character tries to show how cool he is by entertaining a sophisticated party of yuppies with an ostentatious display of lighting his farts.

Even humorist Garrison Keillor weighed in on the subject of man-to-man farting and its flammability in his 1994 *Book of Guys*. Recalling a real or imagined snowy campfire with an all-male therapy group, Keillor describes a bunch of psychically wounded men making testimonials about the difficulties of living with women. Suddenly a burly Russian stands up and proclaims, "I say, nuts to sensitivity. Go ahead and fart. Go ahead."

"So we did," wrote Keillor. "All at once. The fire flamed up blazing bright. It felt good."

The University of Idaho reportedly had a well-organized "cutting" event a couple of decades ago, and fraternities challenged each other for bragging rights. Training required only the consumption of huge amounts of sauerkraut and beer, with maybe two or three pickled eggs thrown in for good measure. The connoisseurs organized an even more elite fraternity, the "Blue Flame Club," whose members not only let farts but lit them. In more recent years, my own alma mater, West Virginia University, several times dubbed America's number-one party school by *Playboy* magazine's college polls, has boasted farting contests up and down its hilly fraternity row. I recall a couple of us trumpeting a few echoes off the hallowed hallway walls of the venerable Woodburn Hall some thirty years ago by holding rolled-up term papers like megaphones to the seats of our pants.

One British campus game is called "making mushrooms": The farter lies on his back and bends his legs way up over his head, exposing his bare ass. A confederate, with both hands full of flour, is poised directly above his anus. Timing is crucial with the mushroom, so the farter must let his friend know exactly when the wind is coming. If the mushroom is done correctly, the flour will drop exactly at the moment of sphincter release, and the burst of gas will create a white billowing cloud that resembles the immediate aftermath of an atomic bomb. English correspondent John Sneddon swears that an old mate named Wiley in Bournemouth was a master of the mushroom.

Most fart fun, however, requires what comics call props. Probably the oldest is the whoopee cushion. In olden times it was called a "fool's bladder," an air-filled balloon fashioned from the bladder of a pig or cow. A jester could harmlessly smack someone with it or imitate a long, ripping fart by slowing letting out the air, stretching the bladder's tiny opening to modulate the pitch. Every kid today still performs this shenanigan with rubber balloons.

But the fool's bladder got its biggest laugh when placed in a chair so that when someone sat down, his or her weight squeezed out the air and created the embarrassing wheeze of a fart. In time, with some refinements, this gimcrack became known as the whoopee cushion. Its name comes from a roughly 500-year-old English word, *whoup*, or *whoop*, defined as a natural exclamation, often ending with an added vowel sound; for example, in 1595, Gabriel Harvey wrote of "The whoop hooe of boyes in London streetes." But *whoop* and the bladder didn't get together until the early twentieth century, in America, after *whoopee* became an all-purpose word for money, sex, or jubilation, immortalized in Eddie Cantor's 1928 hit record, "Makin' Whoopee," from the Broadway musical *Whoopee*. It was in the 1920s that mail-order dealers began to sell what they called "whoopee cushions" in the back pages of American pulp magazines. Whoopee cushions are still sold in magic and novelty shops, but they're little more than cheap rubber balloons made in China and Taiwan.

Bringing medieval fart technology into the space age, a New Jersey company has come up with an electronic, remote-controlled whoopee device variously called the Practical Joker or the Fart Machine. A small plastic speaker that operates on four AAA batteries, it can be mounted under a chair or table with double-sided tape (included in the package); then it's activated with a small radio transmitter from across the room or next door. An alternate version has a time-delay digital trigger of up to nearly three minutes. The glory of this gadget is that nothing is required from the victim other than quietly minding his or her own business. Since the victim is already sitting, nobody suspects foul play from a hidden airbag.

Plenty of other gewgaws make fart noises. Probably the most popular is the razzer, available at any ninety-nine-cent store or novelty shop. Constructed of a flat, hollow rubber tubing attached to a wooden mouthpiece, the razzer is a cross between a whistle and a whoopee cushion and is in fact often marketed as a "fart whistle."

Then there's Le Farter or the Whoopee Noisemaker, a collapsible rubber cylinder, with a hole in the top, that's held in the palm of the hand and squeezed with the fingers, thus creating a fart in the hand (rumored to be worth two in the bush). Next, there's a kind of play dough in a plastic cup—marketed variously as Flubber, Fart Sludge, or Fart Putty—that sounds remarkably like wet farts when poked and probed with several fingers. Flubber, sold by Cap Toys of Cleveland, Ohio, even comes with a warning: "Whatever you do . . . if you're in a situation that demands quiet, such as classrooms, your sister's recital, movie theaters, when dad's telling you 'Not another word!' or anyplace a large crowd can be annoyed and embarrassed . . . DO NOT—WE REPEAT: DO NOT—say to yourself 'Bflatt this!' and stuff your hand in the Flubber pail to make the loudest, grossest, most anti-social noises known on this planet. We beg you."

Then there are the inevitable fart T-shirts ("I Fart Because I'm Full of Shit"), hats ("Hoof Arted"), bumper stickers ("Honk If You Like to Fart"), coffee mugs, greeting cards ("I wanted to give you something really personal for your birthday"—open it up—"so I farted in this card"), plus fart candy, fart powder ("Mix powder into hot drink or food and retreat to safe distance"), a gas shaver (a razor attached to an enema tube; two or three beans are included as "extra fuel"), fart spray in a can ("It reeks just like the real thing"), a fart detector ("Looks like a real fire detector. It really doesn't sound an alarm, but your gaseous guests won't know that"), and thunder underwear (with a hole in the back end—great as a gift but not very practical if you're wearing white trousers).

One of the biggest marketers of these knickknacks is Harriet Carter, a mail-order gift company whose catalog includes Farting Slippers—"Break wind as you walk," says the brochure—and an eight-inch-tall Windbreaking Bear: "How could such an adorable, cuddly plush teddy make such a rude, crude noise? It's the world's first farting teddy bear! Just give him a good squeeze and he lets it rip." (Actually, it's the world's second known farting teddy; ten years ago another company marketed the Gazzbear.) Then there's Bub L. Butt, a six-inch-high plastic man, bent over with his pants down, who blows bubbles out his ass (farting sounds are included).

Some items only seem like jokes, but actually have a practical application. For example, UltraTech Products in Houston, Texas ("the natural gas capital of America"), combines the whoopee cushion with a cigarette filter. It's called the Toot Trapper, a one-inch-thick, activated-carbon and foam gas mask for your ass. Company president Wayne Story tooted his own horn by saying, "I know this sounds strange, but the Toot Trapper's real purpose is saving marriages, friendships and office relationships. With the Toot Trapper, we've created the first chair cushion air filter for people with flatulence." The disposable cushion lasts from six months to a year, depending on how much gas it must absorb.

In a similar vein, a Topeka, Kansas, outfit called NewTek, owned by Brad Carvey, brother of comedian Dana Carvey, manufactures a product called the Butt Muffler, a strap-on charcoal filter. A British company called Farty Pants, Ltd., has refined the design with a "Ring of Confidence" that "uses activated carbon technology . . . and is worn in the underwear [like] a panty liner. The filter affords the wearer and persons in close proximity relief from disgusting smells associated with farting."

The marketplace also has many fart books filled mostly with cartoons and groan-worthy puns. One might even think flatulence has become a literary genre unto itself. For example, there's *The Fart Book*, written by Donald Wetzel, illustrated by Martin Riskin, and published by Ivory Tower in Watertown, Massachusetts. Beginning with the notion that "All farts are divided into two groups—1. Your farts, and 2. Somebody else's farts," *The Fart Book* breaks them down into such categories as the Amplified Fart (made louder by sitting on a metal porch swing or an empty fifty-gallon drum), the Bathtub Fart ("the only fart you can see!"), the Biggest Fart in the World Fart (generally delivered "right in that silence that happens when a room full of people has stopped singing the 'Star Spangled Banner'"), the Did an Angel Speak Fart ("any loud fart in church"), the Dog Did It Fart (self-explanatory), the Fizzle Fart ("always on the damp side and sounds like it"), the Girls Don't Fart Fart ("will shake the walls or blow little birds right out of their nests, but the girl will never give a sign. You are supposed to ignore it"), the Going Up Stairs Fart ("breaks on each step as the farter goes up a short flight of steps"), the Interrogatory Fart ("ends on an up note"—like a question), and the Mud Sucker Fart ("sounds like someone with his foot stuck in the mud slowly pulling it out").

Another fine little paperback is Travis W. Pacone's *I Love to Fart Cookbook*, subtitled *Who Stepped on the Duck a l'Orange?*, published by Double Eagle Press of Arlington Heights, Illinois. Cartoons are intermixed with recipes for such depth-charge delights as Turkey Talkback Stuffing ("This one could ruffle a few feathers"), Roadrunner Salad ("And you thought that was a cloud of dust the old bird was leaving behind"), a Tibetan monk dish called Methane Mantra ("Who stepped on a yak?"), and Swamp Gas Soup ("you'll make the bullfrogs green with envy"). Each recipe is rated on the Fluff-o-Meter, which measures blast, not odor. Highest ranking (8.9) goes to the Cannon Fodder (two mashed bananas, one-quarter cup of honey, one-quarter cup of raisins, one-quarter cup of cashews or brazil nuts, and four table-spoons of coconut), which, says Pacone, "Doesn't look pretty, but if you want to honk with the geese, this is your baby." The lowest rank (1.5) goes to the Whispering Winds Salad for rookies ("Be gentle, this is my first fart"). The book also has a primer on flatulence etiquette and how to blame your farts on pets, other people, a nearby car horn ("Turn and call out, 'Okay, I'll be right out!'"), or a backed-up sewer.

One simple but clever idea is the basis of Philip Cammarati's *Who Farted Now?*, a paperback novelty published by St. Martin's Press in 1991. There's no written copy, only a series of old photographs, mostly from vintage movies, in which people's expressions supply the title's punch line.

If anything marks the recent acceptance of farting as a social mentionable, it's the presence of several children's books on the subject. First there's *Terry Toots* (Chronicle Books), by Francisco Pittau, a story for kids "ages 4 to 8" about Fanny the elephant, whose friends reject her because of her pachyderm-sized poots. Then comes *Body Noises* (Knopf), by Susan K. Buxbaum and Rita G. Gelson, that tries delicately to explain human eructations to children "ages 7 to 10." Its successor is *The Gas We Pass: The Story of Farts* (Kane/Miller Book Publishers), an illustrated primer by Shinta Cho and translated from Chinese by Amanda Mayer Stinchecum, that without apology teaches youngsters about flatulence in a straightforward manner: "The air that escapes through your mouth becomes a burp. When it comes out the hole in your bottom, it's a fart, also called passing gas." There's even a simple diagram of the human stomach. Perhaps the most revolutionary message of the book is: "If you try too hard to hold your farts, your stomach may hurt, you could get dizzy or you could get a headache. So, don't hold them in—pass that gas!"

A slightly more sophisticated kiddy book, Sylvia Branzei's *Grossology* (Planet Dexter, Addison-Wesley Publishing), tries to explain "The science of really gross things!" Fake rubber vomit on the cover removes any doubt about what the buyer will find inside. "Sometimes it's stinky," *Grossology*'s introduction announces. "Sometimes it's crusty. And sometimes it's slimy. But hey, it's your body." Along with barf, boogers, bile, and butt cheese, burnt burritos get several pages of coverage. "You were sitting in class minding your own business, when you felt it in your gut. Rumble, rumble. Oh no! You knew what was to come. You squeezed tightly your anal exit. It was useless: the pressure and then the escape. Flub, flubba, fwwwp: you did it: you farted." There's even a short homage to Le Petomane (though they mistakenly date his act to the mid-1800s), a short list of how to say fart in other languages ("purrd note" in Czech, "dut" in Vietnamese, and "fang pi" in Mandarin Chinese), and how-to instructions on making fart sounds with your mouth or armpit.

Finally, there's a paperback series written by Pat Pollari for preadolescent readers called Barf-O-Rama, from Bantam Books. Two irreverent novellas in the series, *The Legend of Bigfart* (#2) and *Jurassic Fart* (#12), try to live up to the series's warning: "Guaranteed Gross-Out!" In 1997's *Jurassic Fart,* somebody's "killer ninja fart"—or a whirling "farticane" of red zone proportions—sends the boy hero in search of the fatal flatus. "Has the mythic Jurassic Fart come back to destroy humans?" the book asks. "Or did somebody just eat a really ripe piece of cheese?"

Kids, of course, are the fart's biggest fans. In the late 1980s, when cute Cabbage Patch dolls were popular, the Topps company launched a series of bubblegum cards presenting the Garbage Pail Kids, each of whom had a dirty habit like nosepicking or vomiting. One of the card kids was Windy Winston, and you know what his specialty was. (The Garbage Pail Kids briefly came to life in a CBS Saturday morning kiddy show in 1987.)

With today's deluge of arcade video games and interactive computer games, the sky's the limit when it comes to virtual farting. In one video game called *Primal Rage*, for example, prehistoric monsters have the option of fighting each other with their fists or with green clouds of toxic farts (comic books, movies, and video games always render farts as green). An interactive game called *Boogerman* introduces a new kind of hero: millionaire Snotty Ragsdale, who turns into a caped crusader dedicated to fighting evildoers with his "natural defenses" like powerful farts and snot missiles.

Recognizing that computer games are subject to the same parental criticisms as any other amusements available to kids, Sega,

Nintendo, and other major manufacturers of these products established in 1993 a self-regulating entity called the Entertainment Software Rating Board. The board assigned a team of three people to each new game to rank it from EC (early children) to AO (adult only), according to three criteria: violence, language, and sex. But soon the problem arose of how to classify gastrointestinal tomfoolery like burping and farting. One video game that challenged the board was *Beavis and Butt-head*, based on the animated MTV characters. "Being very sensitive to the fact that we don't censor, I said we have a real problem here, because in certain cultures these behaviors are acceptable and even applauded," said Arthur Pober, the board's executive director. He finally decided on a new category called "comic mischief" to describe "gross slapstick or vulgar situations."

Any way you sniff at it, funning with farts is a multimillion-dollar industry, run by people who have bet their respective farms on the inherent humor of flatulence. Their success speaks for itself: Farts are funny.

TERRIER TERRORIST GUZZLES BUD AND GASES BIMBOS

Bull terrier Spuds MacKenzie (actually a bitch whose real name was Honey Tree Evil Eye) frolicked with beautiful women called Spudettes and became an American icon after appearing in a series of Bud Lite TV commercials that were introduced during the 1987 Super Bowl. According to Spudette Lela Rochon (who later co-starred in the 1996 film *Waiting to Exhale*), Spuds turned out to be quite a beer boor when they all went out on promotional tours in a limousine. His farting, said Rochon, was so frequent and suffocating that the ladies in his stable, waiting to *inhale*, frantically rolled down their windows to air out the back seat or else flicked the cigarette lighters they kept handy for Spuds's outbursts.

Incidentally, dogs fart mostly because they eat fast and gulp a lot of air, especially when lapping water. One way to slow them down is to put a tennis ball in their dish. Dry food is less flatulent than canned food. Some dog experts claim that the Boston terrier is the worst farter of all breeds.

13

LEGENDS OF THE FART

Dating rule #1: Fart immediately!
—ex-Playboy Playmate and TV starlet
Jenny McCarthy, 1997

U rban legends are stories that sound fantastic yet ring true because they touch upon one or more of our common anxieties. Invariably a friend or acquaintance delivers these anecdotes to us as gospel, claiming they know the victim personally or else know someone who does—usually their cousin's hairdresser's next-door neighbor's sister-in-law. If these stories stick around long enough, they become part of our folklore. Live alligators flushed into Manhattan's sewers, poodles exploding in microwave ovens, stolen kidneys, green markers making CDs sound better—we've heard them all in one form or another.

Among America's popular urban legends unearthed by Jan Harold Brunvand in his 1981 best-seller, *The Vanishing Hitchhiker*, is what he calls "Surpriser Surprised." The story goes something like this: In preparation for a surprise party, a person is led into a room to await the arrival of the supposed guest of honor. To pass what begins to seem like a long time, this person masturbates, urinates, or commits some other *faux pas* (in one short story, a man even kills his wife, throws her over his shoulder, and sneaks into his dark house in hopes of cutting her up), only to discover that the surprise is on him. The lights suddenly turn on and thirty people shout, "Happy birthday!"

One variation on this theme is the "Fart in the Dark." Carson McCullers included it in her acclaimed 1940 novel *The Heart Is a Lonely Hunter*:

> It was the day of [Biff's] twenty-ninth birthday, and Lucille
> had asked him to drop by her apartment when he finished
> with an appointment at the dentist's. He expected from this
> some little remembrance—a plate of cherry tarts or a good
> shirt. She met him at the door and blindfolded his eyes before
> he entered. Then she said she would be back in a second. In
> the silent room he listened to her footsteps and when she had
> reached the kitchen he broke wind. He stood in the room
> with his eyes blindfolded and he pooted. Then all at once he
> knew with horror that he was not alone. There was a titter
> and soon great rolling whoops of laughter deafened him.

This scenario showed up again on CBS's comedy-drama *Picket Fences*, shortly after its debut in 1992. Actor Tom Skerritt's lead character, Sheriff Jimmy Brock, is blindfolded and left in what he thinks is an empty room, where he farts aloud without realizing a huge party has been assembled for him.

Recent versions of the fart in the dark story have "moved the scene of the shame to a car," said Brunvand, quoting a 1976 story from Utah:

> A plain Jane girl in school, who has never been out on a date,
> no boyfriend, etc. One day the captain of the football team
> asks her to go to a big dance. She runs home overwhelmed—
> has her hair done, new dress, nails manicured, and prompts
> her parents on how to act. In the process of getting ready, the

chili she had for lunch starts making itself known. Near 7 o'clock (the time he'll be there) the gas is getting unbearable. She feels about to bust. Just before she can get relieved, the doorbell rings. She lets him in, introduces him, but by this time she can hardly talk and is breathy. So she begins plotting how to get rid of it before she blows it. So, she plans that when he opens the door [of the car] to let her in, she blows on his way around the car, rolls the window down, fans it out and everything will be fine. He opens the door for her, closes it, and starts to walk around. She lets it out, and it sounds like a howitzer, the windows vibrate, the license plate falls off, etc. She rolls the window down, fans it out, and is all cool and composed when he gets in. He smiles and says, "Oh, I'd like you to meet Ruth and Bob" who are sitting in the backseat.

This story was turned into a short film that airs every now and then as a time-filler on cable TV's Independent Movie Channel.

Another American folk legend is the man who suffocates from his own gas and becomes a "flatality." Occasionally stories surface about a fat guy (usually in a foreign country) who falls asleep in a tiny room after eating a large, sauce-heavy meal and farts unrelentingly until the atmosphere is toxic enough to asphyxiate him.

The *Weekly World News*, a hilarious tabloid spoof that should be required reading for everyone, goofed on this urban legend by running a story in early 1997 called "Man Dies Passing Gas!"—accompanied by a starburst screaming "Flatulence Horror!" Here's the story by reporter Anwar Basarah:

Cairo, Egypt—A flatulent furniture salesman died tragically in his own bed—after he passed so much gas that he suffocated!

The 340-pound man, bachelor Mohammed Al-Assad, was found dead in his small airless bedroom, according to press accounts. An autopsy showed he was the victim of poisoning with methane gas.

"Mr. Al-Assad was a big man with a huge capacity for generating methane gas," concluded the coroner at Cairo District Hospital.

"His diet consisted principally of beans and cabbage and he was well known for his bouts with flatulence. A neighbor reported hearing the continuous sound of material being torn, followed by stifled screaming.

"Tests show that the 48-year-old victim had very low levels of oxygen in his blood and very high levels of methane. Since police could find no other source of methane, we have to conclude it was manufactured by the man's own body."

According to articles in the Cairo papers, Mr. Al-Assad was last seen in a local restaurant the night of his death, dining on a dish of beans and cabbage.

The following day he did not appear for work as expected and his worried employer stopped by the man's small apartment to check on him.

When Al-Assad did not answer his door, police were called and broke into the apartment.

They found the victim spread-eagled on his bed—and a cloud of noxious gas hanging in the air.

"It seems he passed out from breathing the poisonous cloud of gas that hung over his bed," the coroner said.

"Had he opened a window, the concentration would not have been fatal.

"When rescuers broke down the door, all three of them became sick, and one had to be hospitalized.

"It was a great tragedy and a very unusual event, but there was no foul play.

"Death was entirely due to natural causes."

There are also stories about farts breaking up marriages in dramatic ways, though finding more than a few bits of information about them is difficult. Supposedly, in 1994, a marital argument in France over a husband's excessive farting ended in gunplay and death, prompting late-night TV host Jay Leno to deadpan, "You know what's ironic? She could get the gas chamber." A year later, Leno revived the so-called news story and added another salvo: "In fact, she testified that when he lay dying in her arms, his last request was, 'Pull my finger.'"

That same year, reportedly in South Dakota, the state supreme court agreed with a lower court's finding that the fault of a divorce lay with the husband who farted constantly as "a retaliation thing" against his wife. Upholding a sizable alimony payment, one justice is said to have commented, "The price of gas is going up in Sioux Falls."

One visible urban legend can be found in Manhattan's prestigious St. Regis Hotel at the corner of East 55th Street and Fifth Avenue, not far above the sewers where the alligators roam. In the hotel's posh, oak-paneled King Cole Bar and Lounge is a stunning, brashly colored mural of Ol' King Cole, sitting on a pot, that was painted early in the twentieth century by illustrator Maxfield Parrish. By the blissful expression on the king's face, and the tortured looks of those around him, it would appear that the merry old soul had slipped out an S. B. D. Or maybe not. It all depends upon how many cigars and $12 King Cole martinis the beholder has ingested. This semi-hidden wonder of New York City has kept visitors and long-time locals guessing for over seventy-five years.

One of the most improbable urban legends is that an artist

Two gay guys are driving down the highway when they pick up a hitchhiker. After the guy climbs into the back seat, the driver asks him, "I hope you don't mind if we fart up here?"

"Not at all," says the hitchhiker, grateful for the ride.

The driver lifts one cheek as he pulls back onto the highway and his fart goes *Whoooooosh!*

"You brute!" says the passenger beside him. "Just for that, take this." He lifts a cheek and his fart goes *Whoooooosh!*

The guy in back has to fart too, so he asks, "Do you mind if I join the fun?"

"Not at all," they chime in unison.

The hitchhiker raises a cheek and his fart goes *Brrrrrrraappppp!*

The two gays looked at each other and exclaim, "*Virgin!*"

---

once created his masterpieces by farting paint out of his ass. But strangely enough, this is one story that can be corroborated. Artist Keith Boadwee produced fifty abstract canvases "saturated with gallons of paint in a rainbow of colors and an impressive variety of splatters, stains, stripes and runs," wrote a *Los Angeles Times* art critic in late March 1995, after seeing Boadwee's work at the city's Ace Contemporary Exhibitions Gallery. But Boadwee's art, it turns out, was not merely over the top; it was also from the bottom. To create his works, Boadwee had first given himself what amounted to paint enemas and then turned "himself into a human spray gun, squirting colorful streams of paint out of his derriere." In other words, he pooted paint onto his canvases. Lest visitors disbelieve his talents, the "fart gallery" also ran two videotapes showing Boadwee in action.

Though Keith Boadwee has been keeping a very low profile over the last couple of years, there is apparently no validity to the rumor that he was last seen painting elevators in New York City.

While we're on the subject of paintings, there are at least three famous European artworks that contain farts. In 1896 illustrator Aubrey Beardsley etched *Lysistrada Defending the Acropolis*, inspired by the ancient Aristophanes play *Lysistrada*; the lady can be seen blasting a potent salvo from her bare ass in Beardsley's paisley work. Two sixteenth-century artists, Pieter Brueghel (Flemish) and Hieronymus Bosch (Dutch), also included farting in their earthy representations of peasantry. A couple of crepitators are cleverly rendered in Bosch's famous 1514 triptych, *The Garden of Earthly Delights*; at the bottom of the central panel a nude lady is farting red roses, while in the right panel a naked man is tootling air from a flute jammed up his ass. In Brueghel's *Flemish Proverbs* from 1559, a man in a privy is farting and several figures near him (like ol' King Cole's courtiers on the wall at the St. Regis) are reacting with disgusted faces.

There was a time when guys would boast of having seen a girl-and-donkey show in Tijuana, Mexico. No doubt there are clandestine clubs that have put these sordid floorshows on display, but if every man who claims he actually saw one is telling the truth, there must be a lot of bowlegged women hobbling around Tijuana.

Nowadays, according to demimonde aficionados, the Baja California city's must-see late-night extravaganza is the Bite It and Light It Show. The participants are generally two women. One of them kneels down behind the other and plants her lips fully over her girlfriend's anus to await the coming fart. (Within certain gay circles this is called "felching," though the object of their desire is not generally a fart.) Presumably there's been some pre-show ingestion of cerveza, refried beans, and cabbage. When the flatus comes, the fart sucker's cheeks puff up like a bullfrog's—or Dizzy Gillespie's. Then the one who farted spins around, flicks a lighter and holds the flame to the lips of her girlfriend, who exhales a blue darter. Los Angeles filmmaker Johnny Legend, who in 1978 produced and directed *My Breakfast With Blassie*—Andy Kaufman's spoof of the film *My Dinner With Andre*—claims that he has tracked down a south-of-the-border Bite It and Light It Show and will capture it on video soon.

The story of a gerbil getting stuck up some poor guy's ass has become such a staple of urban legend (one Hollywood actor's career still hasn't recuperated from the gerbil rumor mill) that it was only a matter of time before a fart showed up. By early 1998 the following "actual article from the *L.A. Times*" (though no date was given, and I couldn't find it) made the rounds of parties and was posted on the Internet.

"In retrospect, lighting the match was my big mistake. But I was only trying to retrieve the gerbil," Eric T. told bemused doctors in the Severe Burns Unit of Salt Lake City Hospital. "I pushed a cardboard tube up [his lover Kiki's] rectum and slipped Raggot, our gerbil, in. As usual, Kiki shouted out 'Armageddon,' my cue that he'd had enough. I tried to retrieve Raggot but he wouldn't come out again, so I peered into the tube and struck a match, thinking the light might attract him."

Then an unnamed "hospital spokesman" finished the story: "The match ignited a pocket of intestinal gas and a flame shot out the tubing, igniting Mr. T.'s hair and severely burning his face. It also set fire to the gerbil's fur and whiskers which in turn ignited a larger pocket of gas further up the intestine, propelling the rodent out like a cannonball." Eric T. suffered second-degree burns and a broken nose from the impact of the flying gerbil, while his lover Kiki suffered first and second degree burns to his anus and lower intestinal tract.

If you believe this story, you'll believe that farts can fly.

Finally, there's the oft-told tale of the elusive bottled gas of a long-dead notable, reportedly trapped in an apothecary bottle with a stopper or a cork ("the keeper of the fart"). An artist in New York City insists that the sealed vial he paid a high price for several years ago actually contains a fart from Marilyn Monroe. There has also been talk of an Honest Abe fart, bottled some seven score years ago while he was squeezing off a Lincoln log for his family doctor to analyze. If someone steps forward with one of these farti-facts, however, an expert appraisal would be next to impossible and would, in effect, let the genie out of the bottle.

But there is a known example of at least one man who sought to capture farts for science. In the late 1700s, an Italian researcher named Jules-Cesar Gattoni, a student of physicist Alessandro Volta (for whom the electric volt is named), set out to analyze the air inside the bodies of beggars. According to his notes,

> I took a few beggar boys and, by employing a greater or less-er amount of money, I was able to induce them to let them-selves be enclosed in large leather sacks, a sort of leather bot-tle, up to their loins. I then had the sacks squeezed as tightly as possible around their bodies. The better to cut off commu-nications between internal and external air, I had sheets soaked in water sewn to the openings of the sacks, and I left the young prisoners in this uncomfortable posture as long as they could stay. After that I made them plunge up to their stomachs in a warm bath in a tank under a large funnel already prepared to receive the air confined in the sacks (which were collected in large glass vessels), methodically decanting the air thus created for analysis by the eudiometer.

The result of these experiments is not known, but I am no longer drinking bottled water from Italy.

HEY, NOW, WHAT'S THAT SOUND?

There are endless jokes about farts being mistaken for something else. I love the one about a woman who goes to a bait shop to buy her husband a new fishing reel. The clerk, who's wearing dark glasses, tells her, "Ma'am, I'm blind, so I can't tell what model you're buying, but if you drop it on the floor I'll know instantly what kind it is just from the sound."

The lady drops the reel on the floor.

"Ah, that's the Little Kanawha model—$40," he says.

As she bends over to pick it up, she lets a fart.

"That's $49.50," the clerk says.

"I thought you just said $40."

"Well, yes, for the reel," he says. "But the duck call is another $7 and the stink bait is $2.50."

A guest at a quaint little bed and breakfast is soaking in an old-fashioned bathtub when he suddenly blows a humungous underwater fart that surfaces in a series of noisy bubbles. Two minutes later the proprietor knocks and comes in with a bottle of beer on a tray. The guest says, "I didn't order a beer."

"But sir," the proprietor insists, "I distinctly heard you call out, 'Hey, bub, bring up a bottle of Budweiser!'"

Badda-boom!

An American on his first African safari is a bit skeptical about two of his bearers, who are waving their spears in the air and engaging in what seems like a war chant.

"Wooomba!" says one.

"Wamba!" shouts the other.

"Wooomba!" shouts the first man even louder.

His companion becomes excited and pounds his spear on the ground. "Wamba!"

The American sidles up to his white hunting guide and whispers, "Are the natives getting restless?"

The hunter shakes his head. "Naw, they're just arguing over what a hippopotamus sounds like when it farts in a mud pool."

APPENDIX
SOMEBODY STEPPED ON A
DIGITAL DUCK

The Internet is an awesome monument to humankind's inge-
nuity. Its digital technology is a miracle of our modern age,
bringing a wondrous world of knowledge and experience to our
fingertips, yet many thousands of people are using the Internet to
e-mail their recorded farts to specialized domains where they can
be proudly displayed, like a Picasso, for all to appreciate. Internet
users haven't figured out yet how to make their cyber-flatulence
stink, but it does come in all colors and sounds. And like old TV
laugh tracks, many of these farts will remain in the ether of
cyberspace, clapping away, long after the people who created
them are gone.

A recent expedition in early 1998, on various search
engines, turned up hundreds of fart-related Web sites worldwide,
and those are just the ones that have been "spider-crawled"—perhaps by barking spiders. Cyberspace resounds with the ripping
and roaring of razzberry tarts.

Here are the best of the master blasters:

1. The Fart Line
(*www.farts.com*)

Sean Folkson and Robert Appelblatt run this granddaddy of virtual air
biscuits out of Astoria, New York. The first thing that greets you is
"Listen to the Fart of the Day!!!" (Like most fart-related sites,
farts.com contains *wavs*, or digital sound files, and a click rewards you
with the blare or blip of that day's cheezer.) Then you're presented with
the Fart of the Day Guestbook, where you can offer your own comments about the fart and read what other people have said about it.

Then you can browse the Squeak of the Week, where connoisseurs savor the best of the Fart of the Day; the Archives, where Net users send jokes and remembrances of farts past (which have a distressing sameness about them; a budding parodist named Joey pretty much put the redolent recollections in their place by submitting: "One time I farted. Ha-ha, that's funny"); an advice column by Dr. Rex Breefs, the Dr. Joyce Brothers of burrito burners, who claims to be the author of a book called *Flatology and the Risk of Sphincter Damage* that was inspired by the loss of boyhood friend Johnny Ignito, who either blew out his asshole trying to fart a big one or blew himself up when he tried to light one—perhaps the real story's been clouded in history; the Fart Mart, where you can buy novelty items such as the $19.99 Fart-Corder and the $14.99 videotape of *American Flatulators* (a fifty-five-minute *American Gladiators* spoof starring such characters as Gaseous Clay and the Ripper, touring the "Fartland" of America in their "Wind-a-bago"); and the Fart WavPool, the *crepitus ventris sanctum sanctorum*, where the farts are stored, waiting to be let loose.

Folkson and Appelblatt opened the Web site in February 1996. "The farts-dot-com domain was up for grabs and we were able to register it," says Folkson. He claims they get 3,000 visitors a day. "And these aren't kids," Folkson adds. "These are grown-ups nostalgic for their old farts." He updates the Fart of the Day daily, picking the best and the brightest of what people e-mail into the Fart WavPool. "It is really amazing that with all of this technology, people are using it to celebrate farts," said Appelblatt. "They are actually farting into their computers and sending them to us!" Folkson added, "We have 2,000 farts in our database right now." The problem, however, is that people's farts generally don't sound real because of audio deficiencies. Most are recorded and played back on cheap recorders, then transferred—digitized—into their computers' wav files, and finally e-mailed into the Fart Line system. For Folkson and Appelblatt to make all those cyber rumblings fit into their fart file, "We have to compress each fart, and that makes them begin to sound fabricated. With most fart wavs it is just too tough to tell if they are really real," said Folkson. "It's become a raging debate." Remember, all farts submitted become the property of the Fart Line, so if you e-mail one into the WavPool, it's no use trying to get it back.

2. Tracey's Fart Farm
(*www.pins.co.uk/upages/tracey/farts/farts.html*)

This United Kingdom-based page has plenty of sound files and spectacular graphics. As you enter the farm you're greeted by a little man who walks across the screen, drops his pants, and farts loudly, complete with little blast lines shooting out his ass. The little man, it turns out, is an icon available to anyone who e-mails his or her own farts to the farm and "drops" them into the green pastures. For example, there's the "Viennese Waltz—Dropped by Neil," which a little man readily delivers when you click on him (and no, the fart sounds nothing like the strains of Johann Strauss). Other audibles include the "Squirty— Dropped by Psycho Cow," "Fire in the Hole—Dropped by Nathan," and "Beanz—Dropped by Keith." The funniest is the "Famous, Silent One," which, when you click on it, doesn't do anything. There's also a Fart of the Week and a Selection of Unusual Wav Files ("Warning, these wav files are big, but they really are worth downloading and listening to," says Tracey). Since there are no 900 phone lines or merchandise pages, Tracey appears to be on-line purely for the pleasure of trading and listening to farts. Belying the common assumption that farting is strictly a guy thing, Tracey Vee turns out to be a pleasant, thirty-two-year-old British mother of two.

3. Famous Anus' Museum of Fart
(*www.angelfire.com/ca/thefamous1*)

"Years of toil, turmoil, sweat, blood and tears went into the creation of these sounds," Mr. Anus tells the visitor to this clever mix of sound files and graphics. There are a couple of extended forefingers begging to be pulled (clicked on), a photo of a baby, and several boxes containing such farts as "Rocky and Buttwinkle," "Buttweeper," and "Bungroll." If you're looking for farts larger than 32K (requiring longer download time), you can click on the humungous "I have a dream" (180kb) or "Lay it again, Sam" (83kb) flati. Famous Anus is a twenty-nine-year-old, San Diego-based video game designer who prefers to remain anonymous. "To make farts I usually scan the

Internet for various sounds, and every so often I'll find a sound that'll spark my fartistic creativity. I'll take a sound file, chop it up, stick in some gas, and *voila*! Instant humor."

4. The International Farting Society (*www.homemax.com/ifs.htm*)

For a fee this organization will issue an official-looking Fartmaster diploma, worthy of hanging on any wall.

5. Managing Flatulence in Dogs and Cats (*www.petzone.com/petzone/health/cat/20021.htm*)

Dr. Lowell Ackerman, a veterinarian who runs this page for pet owners, says that the biggest fart catalyst in dogs and cats is swallowed air. Dr. Ackerman suggests feeding your pet dry food with low fiber content in large, flat pans, and avoiding vitamin and mineral supplements.

INDEX

BIBLIOGRAPHY

BOOKS AND WORKS

Alighieri, Dante. *The Inferno.* Trans. John Ciardi. New York: The New American Library, 1954.

Anderson, Emily. *The Letters of Mozart & His Family.* London: Macmillan, 1938.

Aristophanes. *The Clouds.* Warminster, Wilts: Aris & Phillips, 1982.

Aristophanes. *The Frog and Other Plays.* Trans. David Barrett. Harmondsworth, Middlesex: Penguin Books, 1964.

Aubrey, John. *Aubrey's Brief Lives.* Woodbridge, Suffolk: Boydell Press, 1982.

Saint Augustine. *The City of God* (Book XIV, Chap. 24). Trans. Marcus Dodds. New York: The Modern Library, 1950.

Baring-Gould, William S. and Ceil. *The Annotated Mother Goose.* Cleveland, Ohio: World Publishing Co., 1967.

Bainton, Roland. *Here I Stand: A Life of Martin Luther.* New York: Abingdon-Cokesbury Press, 1950.

Balzac, Honore. *Droll Stories* ("The Merry Jests of King Louis XI"). Garden City, N.Y.: Garden City Publications, 1946.

Barnette, Martha. *Lady Fingers and Nun's Tummies: A Lighthearted Look at How Foods Got Their Names.* New York: Times Books, 1997.

Barth, John. *The Floating Opera.* Garden City, N.Y.: Doubleday & Co., 1967.

Blake, Williams. *Selected Poems.* New York: Dover Publications, 1995.

Bourke, John G. *Scatalogic Rites of All Nations.* Washington, D.C.: Lowdermilk, 1891.

Bourke, John G. *The Portable Scatalog.* New York: William Morrow and Co., 1994.

Brand, John. *Popular Antiquities.* London: Reeves and Turner, 1905.

Branzei, Sylvia. *Grossology.* Reading, Mass.: Addison-Wesley Publishing, 1995.

Brooks, Tim and Earle Marsh. *The Complete Directory to Prime Time Network TV Shows, 1946–Present.* New York: Ballantine Books, 1996.

Brophy, Brigid. *Mozart the Dramatist.* London: Faber & Faber, 1964.

Brown, Norman O. *Life Against Death: The Psychoanalytical Meaning of History.* Middletown: Wesleyan Univesity Press, 1959.

Brunvand, Jan Harold. *The Vanishing Hitchhiker: American Legends and Their Meanings.* New York: W.W. Norton, 1981.

Burton, Richard F. *Arabian Nights. The Book of the Thousand Nights and a Night.* Vols. 3–6. New York: Heritage Press, 1934.

Buxham, Susan K. and Rita G. Gelman. *Body Noises.* New York: Knopf, 1983.

Chapman, Robert, Ph.D. *New Dictionary of American Slang*. New York: Harper & Row, 1986.

Chaucer, Geoffrey. *The Canterbury Tales*. New York: Modern Library, 1994.

Colford, Paul D. *Howard Stern: King of All Media*. New York: St. Martin's Press, 1996.

Corbin, Alain. *The Foul and the Fragrant*. Cambridge, Mass.: Harvard University Press, 1986.

Dahl, Roald. *The BFG*. New York: Farrar, Straus & Giroux, 1983.

Davies, John. *The Poems of Sir John Davies*. New York: Columbia University Press, 1941.

Delaney, John J. *The Dictionary of Saints*. Garden City, N.Y.: Doubleday & Co., 1980.

Dali, Salvador. *Diary of a Genius*. Trans. Richard Howard. New York: Prentice Hall Press, 1965.

Dali, Salvador. *The Unspeakable Confessions of Salvador Dali* (as told to Andrew Parinaud). New York: William Morrow & Co., 1976.

Doctorow, E.L. *Ragtime*. New York: Random House, 1975.

Dundes, Alan. *Life Is Like a Chicken Coop Ladder*. Detroit: Wayne State University Press, 1989.

Erikson, Erik H. *Young Man Luther*. New York: W.W. Norton, 1958.

Esquivel, Laura. *Like Water for Chocolate*. New York: Doubleday, 1992.

Farmer, John S. and W.E. Henley. *A Dictionary of Slang and Colloquial English*. London: George Routledge & Sons, date unk.

Fielding, Henry. *The History of Tom Jones*. New York: Random House, 1994.

Flavius Josephus. *The Works of Josephus: The Wars of the Jews*. Trans. William Whiston. Peabody, Mass.: Hendrickson Publishers, 1987.

Franklin, Ben. *Poor Richard: An Almanack*. New York: D. McCay Co., 1976.

Ganzfried, Rabbi Solomon. *The Code of Jewish Law*. New York: Hebrew Publishing Co., 1927.

Gardner, Gerald. *The Censorship Papers*. New York: Dodd, Mead & Co., 1987.

Geismer, Maxwell. *Mark Twain: An American Prophet*. Boston: Houghton Mifflin Co., 1970.

Goldberg, Whoopi. *Book*. New York: Weisbach Books, 1997.

Herodotus. *The Histories of Herodotus*. Trans. Harry Carter. New York: The Heritage Press, 1958.

Horace. *The Complete Works of Horace*. New York: The Modern Library, 1936.

Hugo, Victor. *The Hunchback of Notre Dame*. Trans. Walter J. Cobb. New York: Signet Classic, 1964.

Huxley, Aldous. *Do What You Will*. Garden City, N.Y.: Doubleday, 1929.

Hyde, H.M. *History of Pornography*. New York: Ferrar, Straus & Giroux, 1965.

Irving, David. *The Secret Diaries of Hitler's Doctor*. New York: Macmillian, 1983.

Irving, John. *The Hotel New Hampshire*. New York: Henry Robbins/E.P. Dutton, 1981.

Japikse, Carl, ed. *Fart Proudly*. Columbus, Ohio: Enthea Press, 1990.

Jay, Ricky. *Learned Pigs and Fireproof Women*. New York: Villard Books, 1987.

Jenkins, Dan. *Semi-Tough*. New York: Atheneum, 1972.

Jobson, Capt. Richard. *The Golden Trade*. London: Dawsons of Pall Mall, 1968.

Johnson, Samuel. *Dictionary of the English Language*. New York: Arno Press, 1979.

Jonson, Ben. *Complete Poetry*. New York: NYU Press, 1963.

Jonson, Ben. *Selected Works*. New York: Random House, 1938.

Kanin, Garson. *Hollywood*. New York: Viking Press, 1974.

Kant, Immanuel. *Werke in Sechs Banden, Band I*. Wiesbaden: Insel-Verlag, 1960.

Keillor, Garrison. *The Book of Guys*. Hingham, Mass.: Wheeler Pub. Co., 1994.

Langer, Walter C. *The Mind of Adolf Hitler: The Secret Wartime Report*. New York: Basic Books, 1972.

Le Guerer, Annick. *Scent: The Mysterious and Essential Power of Smell*. New York: Kodansha Int'l, 1994.

Lewis, Sinclair. *Main Street*. New York: Carroll & Graf Publ., 1996.

Mailer, Norman. *The Naked and the Dead*. New York: Holt, Rinehart, and Winston, 1981.

Malinowski, Bronislaw. *The Sexual Life of Savages in North Western Melanesia*. New York: Horace Liveright, 1929.

Martial. *Select Epigrams of Martial*. Trans. Donald C. Goertz. New Hyde Park, N.Y.: University Books, 1971.

Maurois, André. *Prometheus: The Life of Balzac*. Trans. Norman Denny. New York: Harper & Row, 1965.

Massinger, Philip. *Philip Massinger*. New York: American Book Co., 1912.

McCullers, Carson. *The Heart Is a Lonely Hunter*. Cambridge, Mass.: The Riverside Press, 1940.

Mennis, Sir John, and Dr. James Smith. *The Muses' Recreation*. 2 Vols. London: J. C Hotten, 1817.

Milligan, Spike. *Adolf Hitler: My Part in His Downfall*. New York: Harper's Magazine Press, 1971.

Montaigne, Michel de. *The Essays*. Trans. M.A. Screech. London: Allen Lane/The Penguin Press, 1991.

Montaigne, Michel de. *The Essays*. Trans. George B. Ives. New York: The Heritage Press, 1946.

More, Sir Thomas. *The Latin Epigrams of Thomas More*. Chicago: University of Chicago Press, 1953.

Nations, Opal Louis. *Etiquette of Flatulence*. New York: Hyena Editions, 1981.

Niebuhr, Carsten. *Travels Through Arabia*. Trans. Robert Heron. Edinburgh: R. Morison & Son, 1792.

Neider, Charles, ed. *The Outrageous Mark Twain*. New York: Doubleday, 1987.

Nohain, Jean and F. Caradec. *Le Petomane*. Los Angeles: Sherbourne Press, Inc., 1968.

Oberman, Heiko A. *Luther*. New Haven: Yale University Press, 1989.

Pacone, Travis W. *The I Love to Fart Cookbook*. Arlington Heights, Ill.: Double Eagle Press, 1983.

Partridge, Eric. *A Dictionary of Slang and Unconventional English*. New York: Macmillan, 1984.

Partridge, Eric. *Shakespeare's Bawdy*. New York: Routledge, 1968.

Peikin, Steven, M.D. *Gastro-Intestinal Health*. New York: Harper Perennial, 1991.

Perry, Charles. *A View of the Levant*, cited in John G. Bouke, *Scatalogic Rites of All Nations*. (Washington, D.C.: Lowdermilk, 1891).

Petronius Arbiter. *Satyricon*. Trans. William Arrowsmith. Ann Arbor: University of Michigan Press, 1959.

Pliny the Elder. *Natural History*. Trans. H. Rackham. Cambridge, Mass.: Harvard University Press, 1938.

Pope, Alexander. *The Poems of Alexander Pope*. New Haven: Yale University Press, 1963.

Promblés, E. Slove. *Fee, Fie Foe, Fum: A Dictionary of Fartology*. Brockport, N.Y.: Melodious Pub., 1981.

Quintana, Ricardo. *The Mind and Art of Jonathan Swift*. Oxford: Oxford University Press, 1936.

Rapkin, Eric S. and Eugene M. Silverman. *It's a Gas: A Study of Flatulence*. San Bernardino: R. Reginald, Borgo Press, 1991.

Rabelais, Francois. *Gargantua and Pantagruel*. Trans. John M. Cohen. Franklin Center, Pa.: The Franklin Library, 1982.

Rabelais, Francois. *Gargantua and Pantagruel*. Trans. Thomas Urquhart. London: J. M. Dent & Sons, 1954.

Randall, Dale B.J. *Jonson's Gypsies Unmasked*. Durham, N.C.: Duke University Press, 1975.

Rawson, Hugh. *A Dictionary of Euphemisms & Other Doubletalk*. New York: Crown Publ., 1981.

Rawson, Hugh. *Wicked Words*. New York: Crown Publ., 1989.

Riggs, David. *Ben Jonson: A Life*. Cambridge, Mass.: Harvard University Press, 1989.

Ross, Thomas W. *Chaucer's Bawdy*. New York: E.P. Dutton & Co., 1972.

St. Jerome. *Select Letters of St. Jerome*. Trans. F.A. Wright. London: William Heinemann Ltd., 1933.

Seutonius Tranquillus. *The Twelve Caesars*. Trans. Robert Graves. Harmondsworth, Middlesex: Penguin Books, 1979.

Shakespeare, William. *The Annotated Shakespeare*. Vols. 1–3. Ed. A.L. Rowse. New York: Clarkson N. Potter, 1978.

Silverman, Kenneth. *A Cultural History of the American Revolution*. New York: Thomas Crowell Co., 1976.

Sinyard, Neil. *The Films of Mel Brooks*. New York: Bison Books, 1987.

Smith, Anthony. *The Body*. New York: Viking Press, 1986.

Spears, Richard A. *Slang and Euphemism*. Middle Village, N.Y.: Jonathan David Publishers, 1981.

Stern, Howard. *Private Parts*. New York: Simon & Schuster, 1993.

Suckling, Sir John. *The Works of Sir John Suckling*. New York: Russell & Russell, Inc., 1964.

Jonathan Swift. *Poetical Works*. London: Oxford University Press, 1967.

Tetel, Marcel. *Rabelais*. New York: Twayne Publishers, 1967.

Toland, John. *Adolf Hitler*. New York: Doubleday, 1976.

Torquemada, Juan de. *Monarchia Indiana*. Porrua, Mexico: Biblioteca Porrua, 1969.

Twain, Mark. *1601: Conversation, as It Was by the Fireside in the Time of the Tudors*. Belpre, Ohio: Blennerhassett Press, 1914.

Van Munching, Phillip. *Beer Blast*. New York: Times Books, 1997.

Vroon, Piet, with Anton van Amerongen. *Smell: The Secret Seducer*. New York: Farrar, Straus & Giroux, 1997.

Waite, Robert G.L. *The Psychopathic God: Adolf Hitler*. New York: Basic Books, 1977.

Wambaugh, Joseph. *The Choirboys*. New York: Dell, 1987.

Wells, Rebecca. *Divine Secrets of the Ya-Ya Sisterhood*. New York: HarperCollins, 1996.

Wetzel, Donald. *The Fart Book*. Watertown, Mass.: Ivory Tower Publishing Co., 1983.

Zacharia, Don. *The Match Trick*. New York: The Linden Press/Simon & Schuster, 1982.

Zola, Emile. *The Earth*. Trans. Douglas Parmee. New York: Penguin Books, 1980.

Oxford English Dictionary, Compact Edition. New York: Oxford University Press, 1971.

ARTICLES

Blair, Gwenda. "The Female Nose Knows Best." *Los Angeles Times*, December 29, 1997.

Brennan, Judy. "'Nutty' Transformations." *Los Angeles Times*, July 5, 1996.

Brennan, Judy. "Stern's New Year's Party Fallout." *Los Angeles Times*, January 30, 1994.

Cerone, Daniel Howard. "Let Buyers Beware: Rating Formulas May Be Complex." *Los Angeles Times*, September 1, 1995.

Charle, Suzanne M. "Flickering Theater of Myths." *New York Times*, September 22, 1985.

Corliss, William R. *Science Frontiers* 80 (March/April 1992).

Crisafulli, Chris. "'Mr. Show': And Now For Something Completely Mad." *Los Angeles Times*, November 29, 1996.

Denicolo, David. "A Pair of Runyon Guys Roam the Serengeti." *New York Times*, June 12, 1994.

Doll, Pancho. "Only a Dad Could Love Some of the Roles Kids Get." *Los Angeles Times*, March 9, 1995.

Freedman, Alix M. "Outside the Gourmet Cognoscenti, It's Just Francophiles and Beans." *The Wall Street Journal*, March 27, 1990.

Gibson, Richard. "Marketing." *The Wall Street Journal*, July 1, 1992.

Gonzalez-Crussi, F. "What the Nose Knows." *New York Times*, January 24, 1993.

Heffley, Lynn. "Videos Offer Live-Action Walks on the Wild Side." *Los Angeles Times*, August 12, 1994.

Higgins, Bill. "A Party So Big It Was Just 'Nutty.'" *Los Angeles Times*, July 1, 1996.

Hochman, Steve. "Whatever: Harland Williams." *Los Angeles Times Calendar,*October 19, 1997.

Hoffman, Jan. "The Rich: How They Keep It." *New York Times*, November 19, 1995.

Ingrassia, Lawrence. "Dr. Colin Leakey, a Real Bean Counter." *The Wall Street Journal*, April 1, 1997.

Jacobs, Frank. "Howard at the Mike." *Mad*, September 1995.

Kakutani, Michiko. "Adolescence Rules!" *New York Times*, May 11, 1997.

Kareda, Urjo. "Is There Any Future For Bad Taste?" *New York Times*, August 18, 1974.

Lamphier, Gary. "Forget the Facts and Give Thanks That All Those Fields Are Outside." *The Wall Street Journal*, January 4, 1990.

Lowry, Brian and Paul Brownfield. "Stern Works Some 'Magic' for Ratings." *Los Angeles Times*, July 4, 1998.

O'Neill, Molly. "Cows in Trouble." *New York Times*, May 6, 1990.

Pagel, David. "The Body Becomes an Art-Making Tool." *Los Angeles Times*, March 30, 1995.

Palmer, D.H. "How Dinosaours May Have Helped Make Earth Warmer." *San Francisco Chronicle*, October 23, 1991.

Parsons, Russ. "The Mystery Bean." *Los Angeles Times*, April 18, 1996.

Parsons, Russ. "Clearing the Air." *Los Angeles Times*, February 24, 1994.

Peterson, Cass. "Cuttings: Not Just the Cow Pasture's Thorny Scourge." *New York Times*, March 24, 1996.

Pile, Stephen. "Ride the Wild Wind." *The [London] Sunday Telegraph*, June 27, 1993.

Rosenberg, Howard. "'King of the Hill' Drawn With a Drawl." *Los Angeles Times*, January 10, 1997.

Sahni, Julie. "Spicey Food For the Bean Wary." *New York Times*, November10, 1993.

Schjeldahl, Peter. "How the West Was Won By Mel." *New York Times*, March 17, 1974.

Sullivan, Walter. "Termite Gas Exceeds Smokestack Pollution." *New York Times*, October 31, 1982.

Sullivan, Walter. "Global Study of Changes in Earth's Livability Set." *New York Times*, September 22, 1986.

Toshes, Rick. "A Capital New Idea for Cushioning the Blow." *Los Angeles Times*, April 8, 1996.

Voigt, David Q. "The Fear of Farting." *Hustler*, July 1978.

Weiss, Rick. "Nothing to Sniff At." *Los Angeles Times*, August 15, 1995.